D0175025

THE JOY OF LESS

A Minimalist Guide to Declutter, Organize, and Simplify

FRANCINE JAY
founder of Miss Minimalist

CHRONICLE BOOKS
SAN FRANCISCO

First edition published in 2010 by Anja Press.
First Chronicle Books LLC edition published in 2016.

Library of Congress Cataloging-in-Publication Data available.

ISBN 978-1-4521-5518-0

Manufactured in China

Designed by Jennifer Tolo Pierce

10 9 8 7 6 5 4 3 2

Chronicle Books LLC
680 Second Street
San Francisco, California 94107
www.chroniclebooks.com

CONTENTS

Let go
like a child blows a dandelion.
In one breath,
an exquisite lightness
and immeasurable joy.

Introduction

What if I told you that having less stuff could make you a happier person? It sounds a bit crazy, doesn't it? That's because every day, and everywhere we turn, we receive thousands of messages to the contrary: buy this, and you'll be prettier; own this, and you'll be more successful; acquire this, and your happiness will know no bounds.

Well, we've bought this, that, and the other thing. So we must be over the moon, right? For most of us, the answer is "no." In fact, quite often, the opposite is true: many of these items–and their empty promises–are slowly sucking the money out of our pockets, the magic out of our relationships, and the joy out of our lives.

Do you ever look around your house at all the things you've bought and inherited and been given, and feel over-whelmed instead of overjoyed? Are you struggling with credit card debt, and can barely recall the purchases on which you're making payments? Do you secretly wish a gale force wind would blow the clutter out of your home, leaving you an opportunity for a fresh start? If so, then a minimalist lifestyle may well be your salvation.

First, let's pull this term "minimalism" down to earth. It seems to have acquired a somewhat intimidating, elitist air, as it's often associated with chic, multimillion-dollar lofts with three pieces of furniture. The word conjures up images of spare, cool interiors, concrete floors, and gleaming white surfaces. It all sounds very sober, serious, and sterile. What role could it possibly play in lives filled with kids, pets, hobbies, junk mail, and laundry?

Most people hear the word "minimalism" and think "empty." Unfortunately, "empty" isn't altogether appealing; it's usually associated with loss, deprivation, and scarcity. But look at "empty" from another angle–think about what it *is* instead of what it isn't–and now you have "space." Space! That's something we could all use more of! Space in our closets, space in our garages, space in our schedules, space to think, play, create, and have fun with our families . . . now *that's* the beauty of minimalism.

Think of it this way: a container is most valuable when it's empty. We can't enjoy fresh coffee when old grounds are in our cup, and we can't showcase our garden's blooms when wilted flowers fill the vase. Similarly, when our homes–the containers of our daily lives–are overflowing with clutter, our souls take a backseat to our stuff. We no longer have the time, energy, and space for new experiences. We feel cramped and inhibited, like we can't fully stretch out and express ourselves.

Becoming minimalists puts us in control of our possessions. We reclaim our space, and restore function and potential to our homes. We remake our houses into open, airy, receptive containers for the substance of our lives. We declare independence from the tyranny of clutter. It's positively liberating!

This all sounds great–but how do we get there? Where do we start? How is this book different from all those other books on organizing your life? Well, unlike many other organizational books, this one isn't about buying fancy containers or storage systems to shuffle around your stuff; it's about *decreasing* the amount of stuff you have to deal with in the first place. Furthermore, you won't have to answer quizzes, make checklists, or fill out charts–who has time for that? And there won't be dozens of case studies about other people's junk; the focus here is on *you*.

We'll start by cultivating a minimalist mindset. Don't worry–it's not hard! We're just going to think about the rewards and benefits of a decluttered life; it'll provide the motivation we need later when dealing with Grandma's old china. We'll learn to see our stuff for what it is, weaken any power it may hold over us, and discover the freedom of living with just "enough" to meet our needs. We'll even get a little philosophical, and ponder how our newfound minimalism will enrich our lives and effect positive change in the world.

Decluttering is like dieting. We can jump right in, count our possessions like we count calories, and "starve" ourselves to get fast results. All too often, however, we'll end up feeling deprived, go on a binge, and wind up right back where we started. Instead, we have to change our attitudes and our habits–kind of like switching from a meat-and-potatoes to a Mediterranean diet. Developing a minimalist mindset will transform the way we make decisions about the stuff we have and the stuff we bring into our lives. Instead of being a short-term fix, it'll be a long-term commitment to a new, wonderful way of life.

After our mental warm-up, we'll learn the STREAMLINE method–the top ten most effective techniques for achieving and maintaining a decluttered home. This is where the fun starts! We're going to have a fresh start for every drawer, every closet, and every room, and make sure that each thing we own makes a positive contribution to our households. We'll give every item a proper place, and establish limits to keep things under control. We'll steadily reduce the amount of stuff in our homes, and set up systems to ensure it doesn't pile up again in the future. Armed with these techniques, we will conquer clutter for good!

Each area of the house presents unique challenges. Therefore, we'll proceed room by room, exploring more specific ways to tackle each one. We'll start in the family room, creating a flexible, dynamic space in which to pursue our leisure activities. We'll debate the merits of each piece of furniture, and figure out what to do with all those books, games, and craft supplies. Then we'll move into the bedroom, where we'll purge the excess to produce a peaceful oasis for our weary souls. Our goal: a clear, uncluttered space that calms and rejuvenates us.

Since so many of us suffer from overstuffed closets, we'll spend a whole chapter dealing with wardrobe issues. (I promise, you'll look fabulous with a fraction of your current clothes.) Then once we're in the groove, we'll attack the stacks of paperwork in our home offices, and reduce the inflow from a flood to a trickle. Our minimalist makeover will tame even the messiest of workspaces.

Next, we'll turn a keen eye on our kitchens. We'll pare down our pots, pans, and place settings, and see how clean countertops and simple cookware can enhance our culinary prowess. After that, we'll take a bathroom break, and while we're in there, we'll cull its contents to create a chic, spa-like ambience. We'll even simplify our grooming routines, so we can make ourselves gorgeous with a minimum amount of stuff.

Of course, we can't forget about our basements, attics, storage lockers, and garages. The stuff here may be out of sight, but it's certainly not out of mind. After we get down and dirty in these storage spaces, clutter will have nowhere left to hide.

We'll also address gifts, heirlooms, and souvenirs. We'll see how these knickknacks sneak into our lives, and devise some creative ways to handle them.

What about those other people who share our home? When it comes to clutter, our family members are hardly innocent bystanders. We'll explore ways to handle *their* stuff, and make them partners in the decluttering process. Whether you're drowning in baby gear, toddler toys, or teenage clutter, you'll find advice for every age. We'll even learn ways to guide a reluctant spouse or partner down the minimalist path.

Finally, we'll explore how being minimalists makes us better citizens of the planet, and helps us conserve its bounty for future generations. We'll look at the true impact of our consumer choices, examining both the human and environmental toll of the things we buy, and learn the far-reaching benefits of living lightly and gracefully on the earth. The best part: we'll discover how saving space in our closets can help us save the world.

Ready to sweep away the clutter once and for all? Turn the page for your first dose of minimalist philosophy. In a few minutes, you'll be on the road to a simpler, more streamlined, and more serene life.

PART ONE

PHILOSOPHY

Imagine that we're generals going into battle, or athletes before a big game: to perform at our best, we must mentally prepare ourselves for the challenges ahead. It's time to develop our secret to success: a minimalist mindset.

This section is all about attitude. Before we can take control of our stuff, we need to change our relationship with it. We'll define it, see it for what it is and what it isn't, and examine its effects on our lives. These principles will make it easier for us to let stuff go and help prevent more stuff from coming in the door. Most important, we'll realize that our stuff exists to serve us, not the other way around.

1
See your stuff for what it is

Take a look around you; chances are, at least twenty or thirty items are in your direct line of vision. What is this stuff? How did it get there? What is its purpose?

It's time to see our stuff for what it is. We want to name it, define it, and take the mystery out of it. What exactly are these things we spend so much time and energy acquiring, maintaining, and storing? And how did there get to be so many of them? (Were they multiplying while we slept?)

Generally speaking, our stuff can be divided into three categories: useful stuff, beautiful stuff, and emotional stuff.

Let's start with the easiest category: useful stuff. These are the items that are practical, functional, and help us get things done. Some of them are essential to survival; others make our lives a little easier. It's tempting to think that *all* our stuff is useful–but have you ever read a book on survival techniques? It's illuminating how little we actually need to keep ourselves alive: a simple shelter, clothing to regulate our body temperature, water, food, a few containers, and some cooking implements. (If this is all you own, you can stop reading now; if not, join the rest of us, and press on!)

Beyond the bare essentials are items not necessary to survival, but still very useful: beds, sheets, laptops, tea kettles, combs, pens, staplers, lamps, books, plates, forks, sofas, extension cords, hammers, screwdrivers, whisks–you get the picture. Anything you use often, and that truly adds value to your life, is a welcome part of a minimalist household.

Ah, but remember: to be useful, an item must be *used*. That's the catch: most of us have a lot of *potentially useful* things that we simply don't use. Duplicates are a prime example: how many of those plastic food containers make it out of your pantry and into your lunch bag or freezer? Does your cordless drill really need an understudy? Other things languish because they're too complicated or a hassle to clean: food processors, fondue sets, and humidifiers come to mind. Then there are the "just in cases" and the "might need its," biding their time in the backs of our drawers, waiting to make their debuts. Those are the items whose days are numbered.

Intermixed with our useful things are those that have no practical function, but satisfy a different kind of need: to put it simply, we like to look at them. Throughout history, we human beings have felt compelled to beautify our surroundings–as evidenced by everything from Paleolithic cave paintings to the pictures hanging over our sofas.

Aesthetic appreciation is an important part of our identities, and should not be denied. The brilliant glaze on a beautiful vase or sleek lines of a modernist chair may bring a deep and joyful satisfaction to our souls; therefore, such items have every right to be part of our lives. The caveat: they must be respected and honored with a prominent place in our homes. If your collection of Murano glass is collecting dust on a shelf–or worse yet, is packed away in the attic–it's nothing more than colorful clutter.

Our stuff can be divided into three categories: useful stuff, beautiful stuff, and emotional stuff.

As you're taking stock of your possessions, don't give an automatic pass to anything artsy. Just because it appealed to you one summer's day at a craft fair doesn't mean it deserves a lifelong lease on your living room mantel. On the other hand, if it always brings a smile to your face–or if its visual harmony gives you a deeper appreciation for the beauty of life–its place in your home is well-deserved.

Now if all the stuff in our houses were either beautiful or useful, this would be easy. But as sure as the day is long, you will come across plenty of items that are neither. So where did they come from, and why are they there? Nine times out of ten, they represent some kind of memory or emotional attachment: your grandmother's old china, your dad's coin collection, that sarong you bought on your honeymoon. They remind us of people, places, and events that are of particular importance to us. Most often, they enter our homes in the form of gifts, heirlooms, and souvenirs.

Again, if the item in question fills your heart with joy, display it with pride and enjoy its presence. If, on the other hand, you're holding on to it out of a sense of obligation (worried that Aunt Edna would turn over in her grave if you gave away her porcelain teacups) or proof of an experience (as if nobody would believe you visited the Grand Canyon if you ditched the kitschy mug), then some soul-searching is in order.

As you walk around your house, have a conversation with your stuff. Ask each item, "What are you and what do you do?" "How did you come into my life?" "Did I buy you, or were you given to me?" "How often do I use you?" "Would I replace you if you were lost or broken, or would I be relieved to be rid of you?" "Did I even want you in the first place?" Be honest with your answers–you won't hurt your stuff's feelings.

In the course of asking these questions, you'll likely come across two sub-categories of stuff, one of which is "other stuff's stuff." You know what I mean—some stuff just naturally accumulates other stuff: like accessories, manuals, cleaners, stuff to go with the stuff, display the stuff, contain the stuff, and fix the stuff. There's some great decluttering potential here: ditching one thing could lead to a cascade of castoffs!

The second sub-category is "other people's stuff." This is a tricky one. With the possible exception of your (young) children, your authority over other people's stuff is pretty limited. If it's the kayak your brother asked you to store in your basement—and hasn't reclaimed in fifteen years—you have the right to take matters into your hands (after a phone call requesting prompt removal, of course). However, if it's your spouse's overflowing hobby supplies, or your teenager's old video games, a more diplomatic attitude is required. With any luck, your decluttering will become contagious, and result in those other people taking care of their own stuff.

For now, simply stroll around and get to know your stuff: that thing is useful, that one is beautiful, that belongs to someone else (easy as pie!). Don't be concerned about decluttering just yet; we'll get to that soon enough. Of course, if you happen to stumble across something useless, ugly, or unidentifiable—go ahead, get a head start, and give it the heave-ho!

2
You are not what you own

Contrary to what marketers would have you believe, *you are not what you own.* You are you, and things are things; no physical or mathematical alchemy can alter these boundaries, despite what that full-page magazine ad or clever commercial tries to tell you.

Nevertheless, we occasionally fall prey to the advertiser's pitch. Therefore, we must account for another sub-category of items we own: "aspirational stuff." These are the things we buy to impress others, or to indulge our "fantasy selves"–you know, the one who's twenty pounds thinner, travels the world, attends cocktail parties, or plays in a rock band.

We may be reluctant to admit it, but we likely acquired many of our possessions to project a certain image. Take cars, for example. We can easily satisfy our need for transportation with a simple car that gets us from Point A to Point B. Why then, would we pay double (or even triple) the price for a luxury model? Because automakers pay advertising firms big bucks to convince us that our cars are projections of ourselves, our personalities, and our positions in the corporate world or social hierarchy.

It doesn't stop there, of course. The compulsion to identify with consumer products reaches deep into our lives–from our choice of homes to what we put into them. Most people would agree that a small, basic house more than satisfies our need for shelter (especially compared to accommodations in developing nations). However, aspirational marketing decrees that we "need" a master suite, bedrooms for each child, his-and-her bathrooms, and kitchens with professional grade appliances–otherwise, we haven't quite "made it." Square footage becomes a status symbol, and naturally, it takes many more sofas, chairs, tables, knickknacks, and other stuff to fill a larger house.

Ads also encourage us to define ourselves through our clothing–ideally, with brand name apparel. These designer labels don't make our clothes any warmer, our handbags any sturdier, or our lives any more glamorous. Furthermore, such trend-setting items seem to go out of style mere minutes after their purchase–leaving our closets packed with outdated attire we hope someday returns to fashion. In reality, the majority of us have no need for celebrity-sized wardrobes, as our clothes and accessories will never garner widespread comment or attention. Nevertheless, marketers try to convince us that we live in the spotlight, and would do well to dress accordingly.

It's not easy to be a minimalist in a mass-media world. Advertisers constantly bombard us with the message that material accumulation is the measure of success. They exploit the fact that it's a lot easier to *buy* status than to earn it. How many times have you heard "more is better," "fake it till you make it," or "clothes make the man"? They tell us that more stuff means more happiness, when in fact, more stuff often means more headaches and more debt. The purchase of all this stuff is certainly benefiting someone . . . but it's not us.

It's not easy to be a minimalist in a mass-media world.

Truth be told, products will never make us into something we're not. Pricey cosmetics won't make us supermodels, fancy garden tools won't give us green thumbs, and high-end cameras won't turn us into award-winning photographers. Yet we feel compelled to buy, and keep, stuff that holds a promise–to make us happier, prettier, smarter, a better parent or spouse, more loved, more organized, or more capable.

But consider this: if these things haven't delivered on their promises yet, it may be time to let them go.

Similarly, consumer products are not surrogates for experience. We don't need to own a garage full of camping gear, sports equipment, and pool toys when what we're really seeking is quality time with our family. Inflatable reindeer and piles of presents do not make a joyous holiday; gathering with our loved ones does. Accumulating mountains of yarn, stacks of cookbooks, and boxes of art supplies will not automatically make us accomplished knitters, master chefs, or creative geniuses. The activities themselves–not the materials–are what's essential to our enjoyment and personal development.

We also identify with stuff from our past, and hold on to certain things to prove who we were, or what we accomplished. How many of us still have cheerleading uniforms, letter sweaters, swimming trophies, or notebooks from long-forgotten college classes? We rationalize keeping them as evidence of our achievements (as if we might need to dig out our old calculus tests to prove we passed the course). However, these items are usually stuffed in a box somewhere, not proving anything to anybody. If that's the case, it may be time to release these relics of yesterday's you.

As we examine our things with a critical eye, we may be surprised how many of them commemorate our past, represent our hopes for the future, or belong to our imaginary selves. Unfortunately, devoting too much of our space, time, and energy to these things keeps us from living in the present.

Sometimes we fear that getting rid of certain items is equivalent to getting rid of part of ourselves. No matter that we rarely play that violin, and have never worn that evening gown–the moment we let them go, we'll eliminate our chance to become virtuosos or socialites. And heaven forbid we throw away that high school mortarboard–it'll be like we never graduated.

We have to remember that our memories, dreams, and ambitions aren't contained in objects; they're contained in ourselves. We are not what we own; we are what we do, what we think, and who we love. By eliminating the remnants of unloved pastimes, uncompleted endeavors, and unrealized fantasies, we make room for new (and *real*) possibilities. Aspirational items are the props for a pretend version of our lives; we need to clear out this clutter, so that we have the time, energy, and space to realize our true selves and our full potential.

3
Less stuff = less stress

Think of the life energy expended in the ownership of a single possession: planning for it, reading reviews about it, looking for the best deal on it, earning (or borrowing) the money to buy it, going to the store to purchase it, transporting it home, finding a place to put it, learning how to use it, cleaning it (or cleaning around it), maintaining it, buying extra parts for it, insuring it, protecting it, trying not to break it, fixing it when you do, and sometimes making payments on it even after you've disposed of it. Now multiply this by the number of items in your home. Whoa! That's positively exhausting!

Being the caretaker of all our things can be a full-time job. In fact, entire industries have sprung up to help us service our stuff. Companies make fortunes selling us specialty cleaning products for every item–detergents for our clothes, polishes for our silver, waxes for our furniture, spray dusters for our electronics, and conditioners for our leather. The insurance business flourishes on the chance that our cars, jewelry, or art might be damaged or stolen. Locksmiths, alarm companies, and safe manufacturers promise to protect our things from theft. Repairmen are standing by to fix our stuff when it breaks, and movers are ready to gather it all up and schlep it someplace else.

With all the time, money, and energy it demands, we may start to feel like our stuff owns us–instead of the other way around.

Let's take a closer look at how much of our stress can be attributed to stuff. First of all, we stress about *not having* stuff. Maybe we saw something in the store, or in an ad, and suddenly we can't imagine how we've lived until now without it. Our neighbor has one, our sister received one as a gift, and our coworker bought one last week; oh my goodness, are we the only ones in the world without one? A sense of deprivation starts to kick in. . . .

So next we stress about how to acquire this thing. Unfortunately, we don't know anyone who will give us one, so we're going to have to buy it for ourselves. We drive from store to store (or surf from website to website) to check out prices, and wish that it would go on sale. We know we can't really afford it at the moment, but we want it *now*. So we scrape up some cash, put in extra hours at work, or charge it to a credit card and hope we can make the payments later.

The glorious day comes that we finally buy it. At long last, it is ours! The sun is shining, birds are singing, and all the stress melts away. Right? Think again. Now that we've spent good money on it, we're going to have to take good care of it. We've acquired not only a new possession, but also a load of responsibility.

We have to make sure we clean it regularly, as dust and dirt may inhibit its function and its lifespan. We have to keep it out of reach of the kids and pets. We have to use extra caution when we use it ourselves, so that we don't break or ruin or stain it. Sound crazy? How many times have you parked a new car at the far end of a parking lot, or had your day ruined when you discovered a scratch or dent? How did you feel when you splashed tomato sauce on that expensive silk blouse?

Then when something goes wrong with it–as it inevitably will–we stress over how to fix it. We pore over manuals or search the Web for advice. We go out and buy the appropriate tools or replacement parts for the repair. When we fail, we drag it into a repair shop. Or maybe we procrastinate because we can't figure out how (or don't particularly want) to deal with it. It sits there in the corner, or in a closet, or in the basement, weighing on our minds. Maybe we didn't break it, but simply got bored with it. Whatever the case, we feel a little guilty and uneasy for spending so much time and money on it. Later we see another ad, and are captivated by an entirely different thing; this one's even more exciting than the last. Oh no, here we go again. . . .

We never seem to have enough time in our days–perhaps our stuff is what's to blame. How many precious hours have we wasted running to the dry cleaners, how many Saturdays have been sacrificed to oil changes or car repairs, how many days off have been spent fixing or maintaining our things (or waiting for a technician to make a service call)? How often have we agonized (or scolded our children) over a broken vase, a chipped plate, or mud stains on our area rugs? How much time have we spent shopping for cleaners, parts, and accessories for the stuff we already have?

We never seem to have enough time in our days–perhaps our stuff is what's to blame.

Let's take a breather, and reminisce about how carefree and happy we were as young adults. Not coincidentally, that period was likely when we had the least amount of stuff. Life was so much simpler then: no mortgage, no car payments, no motorboat to insure. Learning, living, and having fun were far more important than the things we owned. The world was our oyster, and anything was possible! Now *that's* the joy we can recapture as minimalists. We simply need to put our stuff in its place, so it doesn't command the lion's share of our attention.

That doesn't mean we have to rent studio apartments or furnish them with milk crates and secondhand couches. Instead, for now, let's imagine that we have only *half* of our current amount of stuff. Wow–that's a huge relief in itself! That's 50 percent less work and worry! Fifty percent less cleaning, maintenance, and repair! Fifty percent less credit card debt! What are we going to do with all this extra time and money? Ah, the lightbulb's gone on. We're starting to see the beauty of becoming minimalists.

4
Less stuff = more freedom

What if you were presented with a fabulous, once-in-a-lifetime opportunity–but you had to move across the country in a week in order to take it? Would you be filled with excitement and start making plans? Or would you look around your house and worry about how to get everything packed up in time? Would you despair at the thought of transporting your stuff across thousands of miles (or worse yet, find it completely ridiculous)? How likely would you be to decide it's just not worth the hassle, you're settled where you are, and maybe something else will come along some other time?

It seems crazy to consider–but would your stuff have the power to hold you in place? For many of us, the answer may very well be "yes."

Things can be anchors. They can tie us down, and keep us from exploring new interests and developing new talents. They can get in the way of relationships, career success, and family time. They can drain our energy and sense of adventure. Have you ever sidestepped a social visit because your house was too cluttered for company? Have you missed a child's soccer game because you were working overtime to keep up with credit card payments? Have you passed up an exotic vacation because there was nobody to watch the house?

Unfortunately, simply stuffing everything into drawers, baskets, and bins won't do the trick.

Look around at all the things in the room where you're sitting. Imagine that each of these objects–every individual possession–is tied to you with a length of rope. Some are tied to your arms, some to your waist, some to your legs. (For extra drama, visualize chains instead.) Now try to get up and move around, with all this stuff dragging and clinging and clanging behind you. Not too easy, huh? You probably won't be able to get very far or do very much. It won't be long before you give up, sit back down, and realize it takes much less effort to stay where you are.

In a similar way, too much clutter can weigh on our spirits. It's like all those items have their own gravitational field and are constantly pulling us down and holding us back. We can literally feel heavy and lethargic in a cluttered room, too tired and lazy to get up and accomplish anything. Contrast this with a clean, bright, sparsely furnished room–in such a space, we feel light and liberated and full of possibility. Without the burden of all those belongings, we feel energetic and ready for anything.

With this in mind, we may be tempted to enact a quick fix and create the *illusion* of uncluttered space. We'll just nip on down to the superstore, nab some pretty containers, and make a minimalist room *tout de suite*. Unfortunately, simply stuffing everything into drawers, baskets, and bins won't do the trick. Even stuff that's hidden away (be it in the hall closet, down the basement, or across town in a storage unit) stays in the back of our minds. In order to free ourselves mentally, we must shake off the stuff entirely.

Here's something else to consider: in addition to crowding us physically and stifling us psychologically, things also enslave us financially via the debt used to pay for them. The more money we owe, the more sleepless our nights, and the more limited our opportunities. It's no picnic to get up every morning and drag ourselves to jobs we don't like, to pay for stuff we may no longer have, use, or even want. We can think of so many other things we'd rather be doing! Furthermore, if we've exhausted our paychecks (and then some) on consumer products, we've dried up our resources for other, more fulfilling pursuits like taking an art class or investing in an up-and-coming business.

Travel is a wonderful analogy to the freedom of minimalist living. Think about what a pain it is to drag around two or three heavy suitcases when you're on vacation. You've anticipated the trip for ages, and when you disembark from your plane you can't wait to explore the sights. Not so fast. First you have to wait (and wait and wait) for your bags to appear on the luggage carousel. Next, you need to haul them through the airport. You might as well head to the taxi stand, as maneuvering them on the subway would be nearly impossible. And forget about getting a jump on sightseeing–you *must* head directly to your hotel, to rid yourself of this enormous burden. When you finally reach your room, you collapse in exhaustion.

Minimalism, on the other hand, makes you nimble. Imagine traveling with only a light backpack instead–the experience is positively exhilarating. You arrive at your destination, leap off the plane, and zip by the crowds awaiting their luggage. You then jump on the subway, catch a bus, or start walking in the direction of your hotel. Along the way, you experience all the sights, sounds, and smells of a foreign city, with the time and energy to savor it all. You're mobile, flexible, and free as a bird–able to tote your bag to museums and tourist sites, and stash it in a locker when need be.

In contrast to the first scenario, you hit the ground running, and spend the afternoon seeing the sights instead of lugging around your stuff. You arrive at your hotel energized by your experience and ready for more.

When we're no longer chained to our stuff, we can savor life, connect with others, and participate in our communities. We're more open to experiences, and better able to recognize and take advantage of opportunities. The less baggage we're dragging around (both physically and mentally), the more living we can do!

5
Detach from your stuff

Zen Buddhism teaches that in order to be happy, we must let go of our worldly attachments. In fact, haiku poet Bashō famously wrote that when his house burned down, he had a better view of the moon. Now that's someone who's detached from his stuff!

While we don't have to go to such extremes, we'd do well to cultivate a similar sense of nonattachment. Developing such an attitude will make it significantly easier to declutter our homes–not to mention ease the pain when things are taken from us by other means (such as theft, flood, fire, or a natural disaster).

Therefore, we'll spend this chapter doing mental exercises to loosen the grip our stuff has on us. To achieve our goals, we'll need to stretch, limber up, and get into shape for the task ahead. In the next few pages, we'll build up our minimalist muscles–and gain the psychological strength and flexibility we'll need for a showdown with our stuff.

We'll start with something easy to get warmed up: let's imagine life without our stuff. This is a cinch–we don't really have to imagine it, we can *remember* it.

Many of us look back on our young adult days as one of the happiest, most carefree times of our lives. No matter that we were living in a shoebox (sometimes with two or three other people), and had little disposable income. No matter that we couldn't afford designer clothes, fancy watches, or electronic gadgets. All of our possessions fit in a few crates, and we didn't have to worry about car repairs, home maintenance, or even going to the dry cleaners. What little stuff we had took a backseat to our social lives.

Think such liberty is a thing of the past? Not necessarily. Many of us get the chance to relive our "stuff-free" lives once or twice a year–when we go on vacation. The word "vacation," in fact, comes from the Latin *vacare*, meaning "to be empty." No wonder we love to get away from it all!

Think about the last time you went camping, for instance. You carried everything you needed, for both comfort and survival, in your pack. You fussed little over appearance, and functioned perfectly well with the clothes on your back. You cooked your supper in a portable pan over an open fire and dined with nothing fancier than a plate, cup, and fork.

Your tent, the simplest of shelters, kept you warm and dry. Your minimal possessions were in sync with your needs, leaving you plenty of time to relax and commune with nature.

So why do we need so much *more* when we get back to our "real" lives? Well, we don't, actually–and that's the point of these exercises. We'll come to recognize that much of the stuff that surrounds us is hardly necessary to our health and happiness.

Now that you're loosened up, let's kick things up a notch: pretend you're moving overseas. But don't start dialing your local self-storage company–this is a permanent move. You can't just stash your stuff away in anticipation of returning. Furthermore, transporting items across the globe is complex and costly, so you'll have to pare down to what you can't live without.

Survey the contents of your house and decide exactly what you'll take. Would your old, beat-up guitar make the cut? How about your ceramic animal collection? Would you devote precious cargo space to that ugly sweater you received three Christmases ago, the shoes that pinch your feet after fifteen minutes of wear, or the oil painting you inherited but never liked? Of course not! Doesn't it feel great? It's amazing what you're able to ditch when you suddenly have the "permission."

Okay, you're on your game now, so let's tackle a tough one: it's the middle of the night, and you're awakened by the piercing sound of the fire alarm. Holy smokes! You have only minutes–maybe seconds–to decide what you'll save as you head out of the house.

Admittedly, you'll have little opportunity for decisions here, and will have to rely mainly on instinct. If you have the time, you might grab some important files, the family photo album, and maybe your laptop. But it's more likely you'll have to sacrifice all your stuff in order to get yourself, your family, and your pets out alive. In that moment, you won't care a whit about all those *things* that so thoroughly consumed you in the past.

In the grand scheme of things, our stuff isn't all that important.

Whew! Let's take a moment after that one to slow down our heartbeats. Actually, we're going to slow them way, way down . . . until they stop. What?

As much as we hate to think about it, our time here on earth will someday end, and unfortunately, it could happen sooner than we expect. And what's going to happen after that? People are going to look through our stuff. Yikes! It's a good thing we won't be able to blush, because that could be downright embarrassing.

Like it or not, the things we leave behind become part of our legacy–and I can't imagine any of us want to be memorialized as junk collectors or packrats. Wouldn't you rather be remembered as someone who lived lightly and gracefully, with only the basic necessities and a few special items?

Take some time and mentally catalog your "estate." What story does your stuff tell about you? Hopefully, it's not, "Boy, she had quite an affinity for takeout containers" or "That's odd, I didn't know he collected old calendars." Do your heirs a favor, and don't make them slog through a houseful of clutter after your demise. Otherwise, when you peer down from your afterlife, you'll likely see strangers pawing through your "treasures" at a giant yard sale.

All right, I promise, no more doom and gloom–this is a happy book! The point is, a jolt from our everyday routines (be it from a vacation or a disaster) helps put our stuff in perspective. Such scenarios help us see that in the grand scheme of things, our stuff isn't all that important, and with that realization, we can weaken the power it has over us, and be ready (and willing) to let it go.

6
Be a good gatekeeper

British writer and designer William Morris penned one of my favorite minimalist quotes: "Have nothing in your house that you do not know to be useful, or believe to be beautiful." It's a wonderful sentiment, but how exactly do we put it into practice? After all, we don't intentionally bring useless or ugly things into our homes; yet somehow, those less-than-desirables find their way in. The solution: become a good gatekeeper.

The concept is pretty straightforward. Things come into our houses by one of two ways: we buy them, or they're given to us. No matter what we'd like to think, they don't slip in when we're not looking, seeking shelter from the great outdoors. They don't materialize out of thin air, nor are they reproducing behind our backs (except perhaps the paperclips and plastic food containers). Unfortunately, the responsibility lies squarely on our shoulders: we let them in.

As you evaluate your possessions, ask how each item came into your life. Did you seek it out, pay for it, and excitedly bring it back to your house or apartment? Did it follow you home from that conference in Chicago, or from that trip to Hawaii? Or did it sneak in disguised in colorful paper and a pretty bow?

All we need to do is stop and think "Why?" before we buy.

Our homes are our castles, and we devote plenty of resources to defending them. We spray them with pest control to keep the bugs out, we use air filters to keep pollutants out, and we have security systems to keep intruders out. What are we missing? A stuff blocker to keep the clutter out! Since I have yet to see such a product on the market, we must take matters into our own hands.

We have the power to exercise complete control over what we buy. Don't let down your defenses when something slips into your cart–in fact, don't escort any item to the checkout counter without extensive questioning. Ask the following (in your head!) of each potential purchase: "Do you deserve a place in my home?" "What value will you add to my household?" "Will you make my life easier?" "Or are you going to be more trouble than you're worth?" "Do I have a place to put you?" "Do I already have something just like you?" "Will I want to keep you forever (or at least a very long time)?" "If not, how hard will it be to get rid of you?" The last question alone saved me from lugging home a suitcase full of souvenirs from Japan—because once something has memories, it's a bugger to get rid of.

See, that's not too difficult. All we need to do is stop and think "Why?" before we buy. But what about those things we don't *choose* to acquire—and oftentimes don't even want? (Gifts, freebies, and promotional items, I'm looking at you!) It can be hard (or rude) to refuse them; yet once they take up residence in our homes, they can be even harder to evict.

The best defense is a good offense, especially when it comes to freebies. Learning to decline them politely is a valuable technique, which comes in handy more often than you think. Pass up the magnets, pens, and paperweights with corporate logos and accept a business card instead. Turn down the cosmetic samples at the mall (hey, wait—what were you doing at the mall?), and the trial size detergents from the supermarket. Decline the toaster when you open a bank account. And by all means, leave those little lotions and shampoos in the hotels where they belong. Unless you honestly plan to *use* them, don't let these miniatures clutter up your cabinets.

Gifts, on the other hand, require a different game plan. When you're presented with one, refusal generally isn't an option. I've found it best to accept them graciously, without going overboard on the gratitude (otherwise, you'll surely receive more!). We must then focus our efforts on avoiding new ones–by extracting ourselves from gift exchanges–and dealing with those we've received but don't want. We'll navigate this tricky terrain in detail in chapter 28.

In order to be a good gatekeeper, you have to think of your house as sacred space, not storage space. You're under no obligation to provide a home to every stray object that crosses your path. When one tries to sneak or charm its way in, remember that you have the power to deny entrance. If the item won't add value to your life in terms of function or beauty, hang out the "Sorry, No Vacancy" sign. A simple refusal up front will save you tons of decluttering down the road.

7
Embrace space

I hope you like quotes, because I'm starting this chapter with another one of my favorites: "Music is the space between the notes." My interpretation of composer Claude Debussy's words: beauty requires a certain amount of emptiness to be appreciated–otherwise, you have only chaos and cacophony.

For our purposes, we'll put a minimalist twist on this idea and say, "Life is the space between our things." Too much clutter can stifle our creativity, and make our lives discordant. Conversely, the more space we have, the more beautifully and harmoniously we can live.

Space: it's not anything, really, but we never seem to have enough of it. The lack of it distresses us to no end; in fact, we'd do almost anything to have more space in our houses, more space in our closets, and more space in our garages. We remember having larger amounts of it sometime in the past, and its disappearance is cause for concern. We look around and wonder, "Where did all our space go?"

We have fond memories of how it looked the first day we moved into our homes; oh, all that glorious space! But what happened? It's not nearly as impressive as we remember it. Well, our space didn't go anywhere. It's still right there where we left it. The space didn't change; our priorities did. We focused so much of our attention on stuff that we completely forgot about the space. We lost sight of the fact that the two are mutually exclusive–that for each new thing we bring into our homes, a little bit of space disappears. The problem: we put more value on our stuff than on our space.

Here's the good news: space may be easy to lose, but it's just as easy to reclaim. Get rid of an item, and voilà! Space! Get rid of another item, and voilà! More space! Soon, all those little spaces add up to a big space, and we can actually move around again. Take advantage of all that newfound space and do a little happy dance!

What we need to keep in mind (and what is way too easy to forget) is that the amount of stuff we're able to own is limited by the amount of space we have to contain it. No amount of stuffing, scrunching, pushing, or pulling will change that. Seal it up in "magic" vacuum bags if you want, but even they have to go somewhere. So if you live in a small apartment, or you don't have a lot of closets, you can't bring home a lot of stuff. Period.

By the same token, we don't need to fill all the space we have. Remember, space is of equal value to things (or greater, depending on your perspective). If you live in a four-thousand-square-foot house, you don't *need* to acquire four thousand square feet of stuff. If you're lucky enough to have a walk-in closet, you don't *need* to pack every inch of it. Really! In fact, you'll live and breathe a lot easier if you don't.

Space may be easy to lose, but it's just as easy to reclaim.

We talked a little bit about the value of containers in the introduction, and how they hold the greatest potential when they're empty. When we want to enjoy a pot of tea, we need an empty cup to pour it into. When we want to make a meal, we need an empty pot to cook it in. When we want to do the tango, we need an empty room to dance it in.

Likewise, our houses are the containers of our domestic lives. When we want to relax, create, and play with our families, we need some empty space in which to do it. Alternatively, we can think of our homes as the stages for our lives. For the best performance, we must be able to move about and express ourselves freely; it's certainly no fun (nor particularly graceful) if we're tripping over the props.

We also need space for our ideas and thoughts–a cluttered room usually leads to a cluttered mind. Say you're sitting on your sofa, maybe reading a book or listening to music, and a truly profound thought captures your imagination: perhaps you've had an insight into human nature, or are on the brink of uncovering the meaning of life. You're deep in thought, solving the mysteries of mankind, when your gaze falls on the stack of magazines on the coffee table, or the laundry basket in the corner. "Hmm, I really must attend to that," you think; "I wonder if there's time before dinner. . . ." Your mind immediately takes a detour and your train of thought is lost–and with it, your legacy as a great philosopher.

Of course, you don't have to be channeling Aristotle to appreciate an uncluttered environment. Even activities of a more mundane variety benefit greatly from space and clarity; for instance, it's much easier to give your full attention to your partner or toddler when there aren't a million doodads around to confuse and distract you.

In fact, that's the greatest thing about space: it puts the things (and people) that are truly special to us in the spotlight. If you owned a beautiful painting, you wouldn't crowd it with other décor–you'd hang it on its own, with enough space around it to show it off. If you had an exquisite vase, you wouldn't bury it in a pile of junk–you'd put it on its own pedestal. We need to treat what's important to us with similar respect; which, in effect, means removing all the other stuff that's not so important.

By creating space in our homes, we put the focus back where it should be: on what we do, rather than what we own. Life is too short to waste fussing over stuff. When we're old and gray, we won't wax poetic on the things we had–but rather on what we did in the spaces between them.

8
Enjoy without owning

What if someone offered you the *Mona Lisa*—with the stipulation that you couldn't sell it? Sure, you'd have the opportunity to gaze on a breathtaking painting twenty-four hours a day, but suddenly the responsibility of one of humanity's greatest treasures would rest squarely on your shoulders. It'd be no small task to keep her secure from theft, clean from dust and debris, protected from sunlight, and stored at the optimum temperature and humidity. You'd no doubt also have to deal with a steady stream of art lovers wanting to view her. In all likelihood, any pleasure you'd derive from her ownership would be usurped by the burden of her care and upkeep. Before long, that mysterious smile might no longer seem so charming.

On second thought, thanks but no thanks—we'll leave her in the Louvre instead!

We're incredibly lucky, in our modern society, to have access to so many of mankind's masterpieces–without having to acquire and maintain them ourselves. Our cities are such amazing resources of art, culture, and entertainment that we have no need to create artificial approximations of them within our own four walls.

I learned this lesson years ago, when I was fresh out of college. I had studied art history in school and worked part-time in a contemporary art gallery. I attended scores of exhibitions, read dozens of monographs, and fancied myself quite the connoisseur. So when I had the chance to acquire a print by a well-known artist, I jumped at the opportunity. It was a big step in my young adult life–I was on my way to becoming an art collector.

The joy of acquisition waned a bit when I faced the responsibility (and expense) of having the print archivally matted and properly framed. Next, I had to tackle the issue of where to display it. Naturally, I hadn't stopped to think how a modern work of art would look in my prewar apartment. Nor had I considered things such as lighting, glare, and sight lines. In the end, I settled on the place of honor above the fireplace. Although it clashed a little with the vintage tile work, I wanted it to be the centerpiece of my décor (I'd paid good money for it, after all).

Once I worked through these issues, I was finally able to sit back and admire my treasure. Imagine my surprise when one day I spotted a little black bug, smack dab in the middle of my precious print! I couldn't fathom how it had gotten under the glass, but there was nothing I could do but let it be.

Nevertheless, I displayed the print proudly–and carefully wrapped it up and carted it with me when I moved. My new apartment lease prohibited wall hangings, so the print acquired a less glamorous position on the floor. After several more relocations, I became decidedly less enthusiastic about hauling it around and finding places to put it. It spent five years covered in bubble wrap and stuffed in a closet before I finally sold it. From then on, I decided to let the museums handle the art, and I'd go and enjoy it at my leisure.

In fact, finding ways to "enjoy without owning" is one of the keys to having a minimalist home. Case in point: those cappuccino makers gathering dust in our kitchen cupboards. In theory, it seems convenient (and somewhat decadent) to be able to make a steaming cup of frothy java in the comfort of our own homes. In reality, the contraption is a pain to drag out, set up, and clean up when we're finished, and to top it off, the brew never seems to taste quite as good. It's somehow less *special* when we can have it anytime. After playing barista a few times, we realize it's more fun to visit the local coffee shop and soak in the ambience while sipping our drink.

In pursuing a minimalist lifestyle, we must resist the temptation to recreate the outside world within our abodes. Instead of buying (and maintaining) the equipment for a home theater, home gym, or resort-style backyard, go to the movies, go for a run, or go to your local park or pool. That way, you can enjoy these activities without having to store and care for all the stuff.

In pursuing a minimalist lifestyle, we must resist the temptation to recreate the outside world within our abodes.

If you're particularly susceptible to buying pretty things, make "enjoy without owning" your mantra while shopping. Admire the delicacy of a glass figurine, the metalwork on an antique bracelet, or the vibrant colors of an artisan vase–but instead of bringing it home, leave it in the showcase. Think of it like a museum trip: an opportunity to admire the beauty and design of well-crafted objects, without the possibility (or pressure) of ownership. I do the same while surfing the Internet; and to be honest, I get just as much satisfaction from looking at the pictures as I would from owning the pieces.

In our quest to become minimalists, we want to reduce the amount of things in our homes that require our care and attention. Fortunately, we have ample opportunity to do so–

simply by shifting some of our pleasures and activities into the public realm. In fact, it produces a pretty wonderful side effect. For when we hang out in parks, museums, movie houses, and coffee shops–instead of trying to create similar experiences in our own homes–we become more socially active and civically engaged. By breaking down the walls of stuff around us, we're able to get out into the world and enjoy fresher, more direct, and more rewarding experiences.

9

The joy of enough

Chinese philosopher Lao Tzu, author of the *Tao Te Ching*, wrote, "He who knows he has enough is rich."

Enough–it's a slippery concept. What's enough for one is too little for the next guy and too much for another. Most of us would agree we have enough food, enough water, enough clothing, and enough shelter to meet our basic needs. And anyone reading this book probably feels that they have enough things. So why do we still feel the urge to buy–and own–*more*?

Let's investigate this word "enough" a little more closely. Dictionary.com defines it as "adequate for the want or need; sufficient for the purpose or to satisfy desire." Ah, there's the problem: even though we've satisfied our needs, there's still the matter of our wants and desires. In order to experience the joy of "enough," that's where we'll need to focus. It's quite simple, actually: happiness is wanting what you have. When your wants are satisfied by the things you already have, there's no need to acquire any more. But wants can be pesky little things; and in order to get them under control, we have to understand what drives them.

> Once we've covered our basic needs, our happiness has very little to do with the amount of stuff we own.

Let's imagine we live out in the middle of nowhere, with no access to television or the Internet, and no magazine or newspaper subscriptions. We may live simply, but we're perfectly satisfied with what we have. We're warm, well-fed, and safe from the elements. To put it simply, we have enough. Then one day a family builds a house next door to us that's bigger than ours and filled with more things. Suddenly our "enough" doesn't look like so much. Then more families move in, with all different kinds of houses, cars, and things; holy cow, we never realized how much stuff we *didn't* have! A satellite connection brings us TV and Internet, and we get a glimpse into the lavish lives of the rich and famous. We still have the same possessions as before—with which, up until this point, we were perfectly satisfied–but now we can hardly help but feel deprived.

What happened? We fell victim to the classic dilemma of keeping up with the Joneses. Suddenly, we're not measuring our "enough" in objective terms (is our house sufficient for our family?), but rather in relative terms (is our house as nice, as big, or as new as the one next door?). Worse yet, the problem is compounded because the bar keeps moving; once we've made it to the level of one Jones, we focus on the next Jones up. Let's face it, though: there's *always* going to be someone else who has more than we do. So unless we truly believe we're going to become the richest people in the world, it's an exercise in futility to define our "wealth" relative to others. The funny thing is, even billionaires aren't immune to this phenomenon; they've been known to try to outdo each other in the sizes of their yachts. If contentment with stuff is out of reach even at the loftiest levels, then *what's the point*?

The fact of the matter is, once we've covered our basic needs, our happiness has very little to do with the amount of stuff we own. Beyond this point, the marginal utility (or satisfaction) derived from consuming additional goods diminishes rapidly, and, at what economists call the "satiation point," it actually turns negative. (Perhaps the reason you're reading this book!) That's why "more" often fails to satisfy us–and in some cases, can even make us less happy. Consumer one-upmanship, therefore, is a shell game; the only winners are the companies selling the goods. We'd actually be happier, more relaxed, and more satisfied people if we disengaged from the pursuit of "more" entirely.

Cultivating an attitude of gratitude is far more conducive to a minimalist lifestyle. If we recognize the abundance in our lives and appreciate what we have, we will not want for more. We simply need to focus on what we have, rather than what we don't have. If we're going to make comparisons, we have to look globally, as well as locally; we have to look down the ladder, as well as up. While we may feel deprived relative to the more affluent in our own country, we're living like royalty compared to many others around the world.

I used to feel discontent because my house had just one bathroom. How inconvenient when nature is calling and someone else is taking a shower! How awkward to have to share with overnight guests! Then one day a wonderful book came into my hands: *Material World: A Global Family Portrait* by Peter Menzel. It featured "average" families from around the world, photographed in front of their houses with all of their possessions spread around them. If you ever feel the slightest bit deprived, just open this book. It's truly eye-opening how little some people possess; I learned that even indoor plumbing is a rarity in some parts of the world. It gave me a new perspective on my relative affluence, and made me realize how lucky I am to have any bathroom at all.

Now that we have a better understanding of where we stand in the world (and not just compared to celebrities or our neighbors), let's wrap up our discussion of "enough" with a little exercise. It's very straightforward; all you'll need is paper and pencil (or a computer, if you prefer). Ready? Go through your house, and make a list of everything you own. I know some of you are looking at this page incredulously, but no, I'm not kidding. Make a list of every book, every plate, every fork, every shirt, every shoe, every sheet, every pen, every knickknack–in short, every single object–that resides inside your home. Too difficult? Try just one room. Still can't do it? How about just one *drawer*. It's pretty overwhelming, isn't it? *Do you still feel like you don't have enough?*

10
Live simply

Mahatma Gandhi said, "Live simply, so that others may simply live." As it turns out, this may be the greatest incentive of all for becoming a minimalist.

Now that we're thinking globally, let's consider this: we share the world with more than seven billion other people. Our space and our resources are finite. How can we guarantee that there's enough food, water, land, and energy to go around? *By not using any more of it than we need.* Because for every "extra" we take, someone else (now or in the future) will have to do without. That "extra" may not add significantly to *our* well-being, but to someone else, it may be a matter of life or death.

We must realize that we don't live in a vacuum—the consequences of our actions ripple throughout the world. Would you still run the water while you brush your teeth if it meant someone else would suffer from thirst? Would you still drive a gas guzzler if you knew a world oil shortage would bring poverty and chaos? Would you still build an oversized house if you witnessed firsthand the effects of deforestation? If we understood the impact of our lifestyles, perhaps we would live a little more lightly.

Our choices as consumers directly affect the environment. Every item we buy, from food to televisions to cars, uses up some of the earth's bounty. Not only does it take energy and natural resources to make all this stuff, its disposal is also cause for concern. Do we really want our grandchildren to live among giant landfills? The less we need to get by, the better off everyone (and our planet) will be. Therefore, we should reduce our consumption as much as possible, and favor products and packaging made from minimal, biodegradable, or recyclable materials.

Our purchases affect other people as well. Unfortunately, global outsourcing has shifted manufacturing to where labor is cheap and regulations scarce. Whenever we buy something, we need to consider where it was made and who made it. People halfway around the world shouldn't suffer unfair, unsafe, or inhumane working conditions so we can buy another pair of jeans–nor should their air or waterways be polluted so that we can have a new couch. We need to seek out items whose production enriches rather than destroys the lives and communities of the people who make them.

Of course, it's practically impossible to calculate the impact of every item we buy. We should educate ourselves the best we can, but it could conceivably take months to gather the appropriate information for a single purchase. Fortunately, we can do an end run around this issue and still minimize our personal consumer footprints: by buying local, buying used, and buying less.

As we reduce our consumption to save the world, our homes will stay clean, serene, and clutter-free!

Buying local has significant ethical, environmental, and economic benefits. First, it increases the likelihood that products were made under fair and humane working conditions; you're unlikely to find a sweatshop behind that storefront on Main Street. Second, it eliminates long-distance transportation, saving massive amounts of energy; goods that go just a few miles are considerably kinder to the planet. And third, it helps us support businesses that share our values, create local jobs, and invest in our communities.

Buying used enables us to obtain the things we need without further depleting the earth's resources. Why waste materials and energy on a new item when an existing one will do? Instead of going to the mall, shop the secondhand market for furniture, appliances, electronics, clothing, books, toys, and more. Thrift shops, classifieds, and websites such as eBay, Craigslist, and Freecycle are treasure troves of perfectly good, previously used items. Take pride in becoming the second (or third, or fourth) owner of something–it's a financially savvy, eco-friendly way to meet your needs.

Finally, buying less is the cornerstone of our minimalist lifestyles. Limiting our purchases to essentials is the best way to curb the impact of our consumption. By doing so, we can ensure that we, as individuals, are responsible for less resource depletion, human hardship, and waste. If we truly don't need another sweater or pair of shoes, let's not buy them simply for the sake of fashion. Let's think about the resources used to make them, the factories in which they were made, the cost of transporting them around the globe, and the eventual impact of their disposal. Let's base our purchasing decisions on our needs and the entire life cycle of a product–rather than the fact that we like the color or saw it in an advertisement.

As an added bonus, such a philosophy helps us accomplish our other minimalist goals: for as we reduce our consumption to save the world, our homes will stay clean, serene, and clutter-free!

PART TWO
STREAMLINE

Now that we've established our minimalist mindset, we're ready to put our new attitude into practice. The following chapters outline the STREAMLINE method: ten surefire techniques to rid our homes of clutter and keep them that way. They're easy to use and easy to remember–each letter of the word represents a particular step in our decluttering process. Once we get these under our belts, there'll be no stopping us!

- ***S*** *Start over*
- ***T*** *Trash, Treasure, or Transfer*
- ***R*** *Reason for each item*
- ***E*** *Everything in its place*
- ***A*** *All surfaces clear*
- ***M*** *Modules*
- ***L*** *Limits*
- ***I*** *If one comes in, one goes out*
- ***N*** *Narrow down*
- ***E*** *Everyday maintenance*

11

Start over

The most difficult aspect of any task is knowing where to start. As we look around our homes, we see piles of stuff everywhere–in corners, in closets, in drawers, in dressers, in pantries, on counters, and on shelves. We may also have stuff hidden in basements, attics, garages, and storage units; although out of sight, it's certainly not out of mind. If you feel overwhelmed, don't despair–you're not alone.

Sometimes it seems that nothing short of a force of nature or extreme circumstance will clear the clutter from our homes. Unfortunately, decluttering doesn't happen instantaneously; it's something we have to work at, slowly and deliberately. Here's the good news, though: as we get into the groove, we get better at it; and believe it or not, it actually becomes fun!

In fact, nothing prepared me for the rush I felt when that first bag of discards hit the curb. What I expected to be a tedious and rather onerous task turned out to be exhilarating.

I was instantly addicted. I decluttered in the morning; I decluttered in the evening; I decluttered on the weekends; I decluttered in my dreams (really!). When I wasn't actually decluttering, I was planning what I could declutter next. It's as if I could feel the physical weight being lifted from my shoulders. After I'd been particularly productive, I'd twirl around in my newly empty space with a huge grin on my face. (I told you this would be fun!)

Before we begin, let's think back to the first day we moved into our house or apartment. We walked around the bare rooms, imagining what life would be like within their walls. How wonderful it felt to savor the space before a single box was unpacked! It was a beautiful blank canvas, empty and full of potential, ready to be personalized with our own special touch. We relished the thought of a clean slate–what a fabulous opportunity to start fresh and do things right.

We vowed to unpack slowly and methodically, finding each item its own special place and getting rid of anything that didn't belong. We looked forward to putting everything into perfect order. But then life got in the way: we had to start a new job, prepare the kids for school, accommodate guests, or spruce up the place for a housewarming party. We had to put things away fast, with minimal disruption to daily life, and had no time to judge the worthiness of each individual item. We stashed our stuff the best we could and threw the empty boxes in the basement.

Well, now's our chance to Start Over. We're not going to vacate the premises or empty the contents of our houses onto our front lawns. We're just going to redo moving day–but now we're going to take our time, breaking up the gargantuan task into little pieces. We're going to orchestrate a fresh start for each area of our homes. We'll simply pick a single section at a time–as big as a room or as small as a drawer–and Start Over again, as if it's the first day we moved in.

The key to Starting Over is to *take everything out* of the designated section. If it's a drawer, turn it upside down and dump out its contents. If it's a closet, strip it down to bare hooks, rods, and shelving. If it's a box of hobby materials, spill them all out. Tackling an entire room at once is a little more challenging, as you'll need somewhere to put all the stuff you remove; a nearby room is most convenient and will cut down on walking or climbing steps as you put things back. If that's not possible, consider using your front porch, backyard, or basement as a temporary holding area; the effort it takes to schlep things back to the room in question may be all the deterrent you need.

I can't emphasize enough the importance of *completely* emptying the section on which you're working. We become so accustomed to seeing certain things in certain places, it's like they've earned the right to be there (whether they belong there or not). It's tempting to say, "Oh, I know that'll stay, so I'll just leave it there for now and work around it–what's the point of taking it out if I'm going to put it right back?"

Decluttering is infinitely easier when you think of it as deciding what to keep, rather than deciding what to throw away.

No–take it *all* out–every single item. Sometimes just seeing something out of its usual spot–and how great that spot looks without it–will completely change your perspective on it. The broken chair that's been in the corner of your living room for as long as you can remember seems to have staked its claim to the space; it's like a member of the family, and it feels disloyal (or even sacrilegious) to move it. But once it's out in the backyard with the light of day shining on it, it's suddenly nothing more than an old, broken chair. Who would want to bring *that* into their house? Especially when the corner it used to sit in now looks so clean and spacious. . . .

Decluttering is infinitely easier when you think of it as deciding what to keep, rather than deciding what to throw away. That's why Starting Over–emptying everything out, then bringing things back one by one–is so effective. You're selecting what you truly love and need, and it's much more fun to single out things to treasure than to single out things to toss. A curator at an art museum starts with an empty gallery and chooses the best works with which to beautify the space. Well, Starting Over makes us the curators of our homes. We'll decide which objects enhance our lives and put only those things back into our space.

Remember, the things with which we choose to surround ourselves tell our story. Let's hope it's not "I choose to live in the past," or "I can't finish the projects I start." Instead, let's aim for something like, "I live lightly and gracefully, with only the objects I find functional or beautiful."

12
Trash, treasure, or transfer

Now that we've dumped out our stuff, we need to sort through it and decide what to do with it. We're going to separate our things into three categories: Trash, Treasure, and Transfer. For the first, grab a large, heavy-duty garbage bag (a smaller one will do if you're working on a single drawer). For the latter two, use boxes, tarps, or whatever's convenient for the area you're tackling.

Keep an extra box on hand as well; we'll call it Temporarily Undecided. As you sort through your stuff, you'll come across things that you're not sure you want to keep, but you're not quite ready to part with. Perhaps you just need a little more time to think it over. You don't want a few tricky objects to throw you off track or slow your momentum, so if you can't make a quick decision on something, put it here for now. You can revisit it later and assign it to a pile.

Truth be told, you may very well end up with a full box of Undecideds, even after further consideration. In that case, seal it up and write the date on it. You're going to put it into temporary storage: in the basement, attic, garage, or back of a closet. If, after six months (or a year), you haven't opened it to retrieve anything, take it to your favorite charity. This box should only be used as a last resort–not as an excuse to avoid hard decisions. The point isn't to save these items, but rather to save your *space* from items you're not sure you need.

So let's start with the Trash: this stuff is a no-brainer. Throw away everything that's clearly garbage, like food packaging, stained or ripped clothing, expired cosmetics and medicines, spoiled food, nonworking pens, old calendars, newspapers, flyers and pamphlets, junk mail, bottles and containers that can't be reused, and any broken items that can't be fixed or aren't worth fixing. If it's not good enough for Goodwill, it belongs in this pile.

And I know you know that when I say "throw away," I mean "recycle if possible." While tossing things in the trash is easy, we must keep the environment in mind. I don't think any of us want to be responsible for something sitting in a landfill for the next hundred years. So err on the side of good karma and recycle what you can: most communities will accept cardboard, paper, glass, metal, and some plastics. Of course, before you pitch anything, consider if someone else can use it; if so, put it in the Transfer pile instead. It's always better to send something to a good home rather than to a landfill or recycling plant–even if it takes a little more time and effort. We have to take responsibility for the entire life cycle of the things we buy, including their proper disposal. Be mindful of these issues when you're shopping–it's actually a pretty effective way to curb impulse purchases.

Be generous! Something that's been sitting in your house, unused and unloved, may bring a great deal of joy to someone else.

The Treasure pile is for the items you'll keep, and should contain just what the name implies: the things you truly cherish, for either their beauty or their functionality. If you haven't used something in over a year, it probably doesn't belong here. Consider giving it to someone with more use for it, or if you have that much difficulty parting with it, put it in the Temporarily Undecided box. We don't want to devote valuable space to unused stuff; we want to save it for the good stuff! Ditto for knickknacks, collectibles, and other decorations: if you're not displaying them proudly and prominently and if you don't derive true pleasure from their presence, send them off to a new home where they'll get the attention they deserve.

Finally, let's discuss the Transfer pile. In here belong all those perfectly good items that are no longer good for *you*. Don't feel guilty about letting them go; set them free, and give them a new lease on life. Above all, resist the urge to hold on to something because you "might need it" someday–if you haven't needed it yet, you likely never will. If by some chance you did, would you even be able to find it? Would it be in usable condition? Or would you probably run out and buy a shiny new one anyway? If it's easily obtainable or replaceable, better to let someone else use it now than keep it waiting in the wings for a day that may never come.

As you're sorting, divide the Transfer pile into Give Away and Sell sections. Be generous! Something that's been sitting in your house, unused and unloved, may bring a great deal of joy to someone else. Make their day, and give yourself a pat on the back. Knowing that you're doing good can make it much easier to part with your stuff. If you don't have a specific recipient in mind for an item, offer it up on Freecycle. Simply list the things you're giving away, and interested parties will contact you to retrieve them. Alternatively, give seldom-used items to someone who'll use them more–like your power saw to a woodworking neighbor, or your sewing machine to a seamstress cousin–with the understanding that you can borrow them if the need arises.

Don't worry, you don't have to spend weeks putting your possessions up for adoption. If you don't have the time or inclination to find them specific homes, charitable organizations accept a wide range of goods. Goodwill, the Salvation Army, the Red Cross, religious organizations, homeless shelters, domestic violence shelters, thrift stores, and senior centers are well-equipped to distribute your donations to those who need them most. Your castoffs can do a world of good in your own community: consider giving books to your local library, office supplies to your children's school, pet items to an animal shelter, and professional clothing to Dress for Success. You may be able to take a tax deduction for your generosity, so keep a list of donated items and their values, and obtain a receipt from the organization.

Selling your stuff can also ease separation anxiety. Sometimes it's much easier to let something go when you can get some (or all) of your money back. In fact, the cash may bring you more happiness than the item itself! You have a choice of outlets through which to peddle your unwanted wares, from the traditional to the high-tech. If your castoffs are large in quantity and low in value, hold a garage or yard sale, or send them to a consignment shop. To unload more unique, collectible, or expensive items, turn to the Internet: try online classifieds like Craigslist or auction sites like eBay. You can also sell used books, CDs, DVDs, video games, and other goods online.

Now that you've set up your sorting system, and you know what goes where, you can get to the business of clearing out some stuff. Focus like a laser beam, and declutter the drawer, closet, or room you chose to Start Over. Have fun with it–put on some upbeat music, dance around your piles, and kiss those castoffs goodbye! Once you've assigned every item to a category, those Trash and Transfer piles get a one-way ticket out of the house–and you're that much closer to living only with your Treasures.

13
Reason for each item

As you sort through your items, stop and question each one headed for your Treasure pile. Nothing gets a free pass! Put on your gatekeeper cap and conduct an entry interview with each item. Make sure it has a good Reason for being part of your household: you use it often, it makes your life easier, you find it beautiful, it would be difficult to replace, it's multi-functional, it saves you time, it's a cherished part of your heritage or family. Just because it's a stray (the tote bag that followed you home from a business conference), or seeking asylum from another home (the dishware your sister unloaded on you), doesn't grant it clearance. It must make a positive contribution to be considered for residency.

Some items have strong credentials for staying in your home, but are identical (or nearly so) to something else you own. How did multiple versions enter your household in the first place? Some may have been gifts, but others were likely replacements–in other words, you bought something new, but still kept the old. You bought a new TV and put the old one in the bedroom; you bought a new dining table and stored the former in the basement; you bought new shoes and saved the grungy pair for a rainy day. Save the best, and declutter the rest.

> We could get by with just a fifth of our current possessions and hardly notice a difference.

Other common duplicates are sold in excessive quantities: paperclips, rubber bands, and bobby pins come to mind. Still others–like pens, buttons, and safety pins–seem to multiply of their own accord. The extras end up in the back of a drawer until the end of time, no questions asked. But let's shake things up: if you can't envision yourself ever using a thousand paperclips, or a hundred safety pins, retain just a reasonable amount. If you only need a handful, why keep a bucketful?

Once you've dealt with the duplicates, scrutinize the remaining candidates. As you consider each one, ask what it's used for and how often you use it (if you can't answer those two questions, it shouldn't be anywhere near your Treasure pile). Have you used it in the past year? Do you expect to use it in the near future? Does it make your life easier, more beautiful, or more pleasurable? How? Is it hard to maintain or clean, and if so, is it worth the effort? Would it be difficult or expensive to replace? Would you take it with you if you were moving? How would your life change if you didn't own it? And finally, ask this question: what is more valuable to you—the item or the space it occupies?

If you're finding it hard to make decisions, recruit an objective friend to help. Explaining to someone else the reason why you're keeping something can be difficult, illuminating . . . and sometimes a little embarrassing! What seems perfectly legitimate in your head can sound ridiculous when spoken aloud. ("I might need this feather boa if I moonlight as a cabaret singer.") Furthermore, when there's a third party present, your pride will kick in—and you'll be much less likely to squirrel away something old and ratty. Don't enlist the help of a packrat or sentimental type, though—unless you think they'll cart away some of your rejects!

As we determine what belongs in our Treasure piles, we should keep the Pareto principle (also known as the 80/20 rule) in mind. In this context, it means we use 20 percent of our stuff 80 percent of the time. Read that again, closely: *we use 20 percent of our stuff 80 percent of the time.* That means we could get by with just a fifth of our current possessions and hardly notice a difference. Woo-hoo! This is going to be easier than we thought! If we rarely use most of our stuff, we should have no problem paring down to the essentials. All we have to do is identify our 20 percent, and we'll be well on our way to becoming minimalists.

14
Everything in its place

A place for everything, and Everything In Its Place. Memorize this mantra, repeat it often, sing it out loud, say it in your sleep–it's one of the most important minimalist principles. When each thing you own has a designated spot (ideally in a drawer, cupboard, or container), stray items won't wander your household and congregate as clutter. With this system in place, you can easily spy something that doesn't belong–and immediately escort it out of your home.

When assigning a place to each item, consider where, and how often, you use it. On the broadest level, your house is divided into rooms.These in turn consist of smaller areas like cleaning, preparation, and eating areas within the kitchen, or television, hobby, and computer areas in the family room. An item's ideal place depends on the area in which you use it and how accessible it needs to be.

Is the item in question used daily, weekly, monthly, once a year, or less? The answer determines whether it belongs in your Inner Circle, Outer Circle, or Deep Storage.

Your Inner Circle is the space to keep frequently used items–like your toothbrush, laptop, utensils, and underwear–within easy reach. You want to be able to access such things without bending, stretching, struggling, or moving other things out of the way to retrieve them. This not only makes them easy to find and access, it makes them easy to put away. Remember the Pareto principle? Well, your Inner Circle should hold the 20 percent of things you use 80 percent of the time.

Your Outer Circle is a little more difficult to reach, and should be reserved for things that are used less often. It includes higher and lower shelves, out-of-the-way closets, upper cabinets, and under the bed. Use these places to store backups of toiletries and cleaning supplies, infrequently worn clothing, wrapping paper and ribbons, specialty pots and cooking supplies, and the myriad other things that aren't part of your regular routine. A good rule of thumb: if it's used less than once a week, but more than once a year, your Outer Circle is where it belongs.

Deep Storage is typically outside of your living space and includes attics, basements, and garages. This is where to stash your spare parts, seasonal decorations, old paperwork and tax returns, and other things you use once a year or less.

However, don't make Deep Storage a catch-all for everything that doesn't fit in your house; try to keep it lean. If you never use or look at the item in question, and it's not a financial or legal document that must be kept indefinitely, out it goes. Sometimes the best place for something is somebody else's house.

Keep in mind that "a place for everything" applies to decorative items as well. If an item is truly special to you, establish a proper and prominent place to display it. It doesn't deserve to be pushed aside, around, and out of the way, or to fight for position in a crowd of clutter. And it certainly shouldn't be stuffed in a box in the basement! The whole point of a decorative item is to be able to *see* it; so if you're storing any such things (other than seasonal items) out of sight, it's time to question why you're keeping them at all.

Once you've designated a place for everything, don't forget about the second part: always return everything to its place. What's the use of having assigned seats, when everything's lounging all over the house? To this end, it helps to label shelves, drawers, and boxes with their appropriate contents. Then everyone will know exactly where to put something after they've finished using it—and you'll be less likely to find the corkscrew holed up in the sock drawer, or the stapler getting cozy with the baking supplies.

Get yourself, and your family members, into the habit of putting things away. A neat household gives clutter fewer places to hide. Hang up your clothes (or put them in the hamper) after you undress, rather than piling them on the floor or chair. Put spices, condiments, and utensils back where they belong, instead of leaving them out on the counter. Keep shoes in a designated spot, rather than scattered throughout the house. Return books to their shelves, and magazines to their rack. Encourage children to pick up their toys, and put them away, when playtime is over.

Clutter is a social creature;
it's never alone for long.

In fact, whenever you leave a room, collect any stray items and return them to their rightful place. This simple habit takes only a few minutes out of your day, but makes a huge difference in your household. Clutter is a social creature; it's never alone for long. Let a few pieces hang out in your living room, one thing leads to another, and before long it's a full-fledged party! If things are regularly returned to their spots, however, stray items never get settled.

Now I know that some of you with less-than-adequate storage space are probably crying foul. How can you be expected to put Everything In Its Place, when you don't have enough places to put them? Don't despair—*you're the lucky ones!* The more space we have to put things, the more things we tend to keep–things we don't always need. Those with walk-in closets and extra cupboards must summon up extra motivation to declutter; while you, on the other hand, get the benefit of a little tough love. Having less space is an asset, not a liability, and puts you on the fast track to becoming a minimalist.

15
All surfaces clear

Horizontal surfaces are a magnet for clutter. Walk in your front door with your hands full, and I guarantee the contents will land on the first available surface. Their large, flat expanses are an irresistible invitation to stray items; you can almost feel the gravitational pull.

Take a look around at the surfaces in your house. Is there anything on your dining table besides plates, flatware, and perhaps a centerpiece? Is your coffee table free of objects, save any drinks or snacks currently being consumed? Do your end tables hold anything other than lamps, or maybe the remote control? How about your bed? Are its contents limited to the sheets, blankets, and pillows you'll use tonight? Are your kitchen counters completely clear, ready for the preparation and serving of your next meal? How much of your desk can you still see?

Unless you're already a full-fledged, dyed-in-the-wool minimalist (or an exceptionally good housekeeper), you're likely struggling with some sort of surface problem. It may be confined to one area, like your desk or workspace; or perhaps it's affecting all the tables and counters in the house. It may be a recent phenomenon, caused by something like an upsurge in your children's craft activities, or a pile of work you brought home from the office. On the other hand, the problem may have been building for weeks, months, or even years.

Surfaces are not for storage.

What's the big deal, you ask? Well, if we don't have clear surfaces, we don't have space to *do* anything. Clear surfaces are full of potential and possibility; they're where the magic happens! Think of all the things we can't do when our surfaces are cluttered: we don't have room to prepare a delicious dinner, and we don't have a place to sit down with our families and enjoy it. We don't have a spot to pay our bills, do our homework, or enjoy our hobbies. In some cases, we may not even have a place to lie down at the end of the day.

Never fear! All we need to conquer our surface clutter is a new attitude and enthusiastic adherence to the following principle: *surfaces are not for storage.* Rather, surfaces are for activity, and should be kept clear at all other times. Put this minimalist principle into practice, and you'll be thrilled with the results: not only will your home look neater, more organized, and more serene, it'll be infinitely more useful and easier to clean.

To achieve this, we have to change the way we think about surfaces–in particular, how we imagine their physical properties. By nature, surfaces are "sticky"–they're big, flat, and extremely adept at providing a resting place for items. Once an object lands on one, it's liable to stay there for days, weeks, or even months. Sometimes it stays there so long, we don't even notice it anymore. We grow accustomed to its presence, and it becomes part of the landscape. Another one joins it, and so on, and so on. Before we know it, our surfaces are no longer smooth, but a bumpy terrain consisting of items that got "stuck" to them.

Instead, we need to imagine our surfaces as slippery. If they were slick as ice, or tilted just a few degrees, nothing would be able to stay on them for very long. We'd be able to do our business, but then anything left over would slide right off. Until someone invents such a "magic" minimalist countertop, we'll just have to *pretend* that's how our surfaces function. To wit: everything we place on our "slippery" surfaces leaves with us when we leave the room. If we put a cup on the coffee table, a book on an end table, or a craft project on the dining table, we pick it up and take it with us when we make our exit–and encourage family members to do the same.

The only exceptions: those items whose "place" is on that particular surface–such as the centerpiece and candlesticks on your dining table, or the reading lamps on your end tables. This special dispensation also covers the remote control on your coffee table, the cookie jar on your kitchen counter, and the alarm clock on your nightstand. If you choose to keep such functional or decorative items on your tables, however, limit yourself to three permanent items per surface. That'll keep clutter from gathering in these spots.

Finally, don't forget about the biggest surface of all: the floor! It presents a particular challenge, simply because there's *so much* of it. When our tables, closets, and drawers are full–or when we just don't feel like putting things away–our next inclination is to pile them on the floor. Don't give in to the temptation! The floor has no strict boundaries (nothing's going to fall off of it), so once stuff lands on it, it tends to spread . . . and spread . . . and spread. I've been in houses where the floors are completely buried, save a narrow path to walk through the room. You can hardly move–let alone accomplish anything productive–in such an environment. Reserve your floors for feet and furniture, and keep them free of anything else.

After we've made the effort to declutter our surfaces, we have great incentive to keep them that way. Who wants to repeat all that hard work? The most effective way to maintain them is to develop the habit of scanning them. Before you leave a room or turn out the lights, survey the tables, the countertops, and the floor. If they're not as "smooth" as they should be, spend a few minutes clearing them of their contents. This quick and easy act goes a long way toward keeping your home clutter-free. Heed this rule: if the room is empty, the surfaces should be, too.

16
Modules

In this section, we're going to learn a valuable organizational technique that combats clutter, keeps our stuff under control, and helps us achieve our minimalist goals. It's time to sort our stuff into "Modules." The concept of Modules comes from systems design; basically, it means dividing a complex system into smaller, task-specific components. A computer program, for example, might consist of millions of commands. To keep track of them, programmers arrange them into Modules–sets of related instructions that perform particular tasks. That way, the commands can be "stored" more efficiently and moved around easily in the program.

Well, our households are also pretty complex systems, with lots of things to store and keep track of. They could certainly benefit from a more efficient arrangement of stuff–so let's take this Module concept and run with it. For our purposes, a Module is a set of related items that perform a particular task (like paying the bills or decorating a cake). To create them, we'll need to gather things of similar functions together, eliminate the excess, and make sure they're easy to access and move around when needed. In short, we'll need to consolidate, cull, and contain our stuff.

The first step is to consolidate like items. Store all similar (or related) things together: DVDs, extension cords, paper-clips, first aid supplies, craft materials, hardware, photos, spices, and more–you get the idea. Consolidating your stuff makes it much easier to find things. When you're in need of a bandage, you won't have to tear the bathroom cabinets apart; just go straight to the first aid Module. When you want to watch your favorite DVD, you won't have to scour the shelves, rummage through the bedrooms, or crawl under the couch to find it; it'll be waiting for you in the DVD Module. When you're looking for a certain size screw to make a home repair, you won't have to launch a search expedition in the basement; simply go to the appropriate hardware Module and pluck it from the pile.

Even more important, consolidating your stuff lets you see *how much you have*. When you've gathered all sixty-three ballpoint pens into one place, you know you don't need to buy another. Nor will you splurge on another pair of earrings when faced with a pile of fifteen others. This technique is particularly suited to curbing the accumulation of craft materials, which seem to grow unchecked if scattered throughout the house; in fact, the effect of seeing them all together can be quite sobering. ("How on earth did I get all this yarn?") It'll also keep you from inadvertently bringing home duplicates of things you already own. How many times have you run out to buy something, only to find later you already had one? Being able to quickly check the appropriate Module for it can eliminate lots of unnecessary clutter and expense.

Now for the task all you budding minimalists have been waiting for: once you've gathered like items together, it's time to cull them. As you consolidate, you'll undoubtedly come across excess supplies of certain items; cut them down to what you actually use now and can realistically use in the future. Few of us will ever need all the twist ties, chopsticks, and matchbooks lurking in our junk drawers; set some of them free, and reclaim the space. Likewise, why keep all sixty-three pens when ten are more than enough? How many can you write with at one time, anyway? Consider how long it takes to use up a pen: if each one lasts six months, you have a thirty-year supply–most of which will have dried up by the time you touch them to paper. Go through your collection, and save only your favorites. Apply the same principle to socks, t-shirts, coffee cups, plastic containers, hand towels, and anything else you have in abundance.

Finally, once we've consolidated and culled our items, we need to contain them; this step keeps them from spreading throughout the house again. The container can be a drawer, shelf, box, plastic storage bin, ziplock bag–whatever's appropriate for the size and quantity of the contents. I prefer transparent containers, since you can see what's inside without opening them. If you're using opaque ones, label or color code them for easy identification.

Consolidating your stuff lets you see *how much you have.*

The advantage of using physical containers is their portability. Suppose that while watching a movie with your family, you'd like to work on your knitting. Simply retrieve the knitting Module, and you're ready to go. When you're finished, you'll have little temptation to leave your supplies on the coffee table; just pop them back into the container for instant cleanup. If you lack a dedicated office space, keep your checkbook, calculator, pens, and other implements in an office Module–and tote it into the dining room, kitchen, or other space when it's time to pay bills. Teach your children to do the same with their toys, books, and games, and you'll have much less picking up to do at the end of the day.

I'd like to emphasize the importance of consolidating and culling your stuff *before* containing it. All too often, when we get the urge to simplify, we run out to our nearest organizational superstore and bring home a trunkful of pretty containers. We think that by arranging our stuff into neat little bins, we can automatically create a sense of order and serenity. But if we haven't first weeded out the Treasures from the Trash, we're spinning our wheels. The containers may make our houses look tidy, but they serve no higher purpose than to hide our junk. Instead of simplifying our homes (and our lives), we're merely arranging our clutter.

Instead, declutter as much as you possibly can before putting anything into a box. Pare down to the essentials first, and *then* find a convenient way to house them. Being a minimalist means going one step beyond simply straightening up and organizing our homes. In creating our Modules, we're establishing a system that eliminates and discourages excess—making our possessions equivalent to our needs, and then literally putting a lid on them.

17
Limits

Minimalist living means keeping our possessions in check, and the most effective way to do this is by establishing Limits. Okay, I can hear you thinking, "Whoa, wait a second! Limits? I didn't sign up for that. I don't want to feel deprived of anything. . . ." No need to worry—the Limits are for your stuff, not you! They help you gain the upper hand over your things, so you have more power, more control, and more space. Limits work *for you,* not against you.

Let's use books as an example: we're all familiar with how quickly they can accumulate. We buy one, we read it, and somehow it earns a permanent spot in our collection—no matter whether we liked it or ever intend to crack it open again. We reason that we paid good money for it, and devoted time and effort to it, so we may as well have something to show for it. Sometimes we'll keep a tome just to prove we read it. (Time to fess up: who has *War and Peace* on their bookshelf?) Instead, limit your collection to your favorite titles, and put the excess back in circulation: donate them to your local library or pass them on to friends and family.

Limits also help tame those ever-multiplying craft and hobby supplies. Whether you're a beader, knitter, scrapbooker, model builder, woodworker, or soapmaker, limit your materials to *one* storage bin. When it starts to overflow, use up some of your old stash before acquiring anything new—it's great motivation to finish the projects you've started. Not only does it reduce your clutter, it's a good reality check: do you enjoy doing the craft as much as collecting the materials for it? If not, perhaps you should rethink your hobby, and if so, you should have no problem using up those supplies.

You may initially think that Limits will be stifling; but you'll soon discover that they're absolutely liberating!

Limits can, and should, be applied to just about everything. Have fun setting boundaries for your stuff: require that all your DVDs fit on their assigned shelf, all your sweaters in their designated drawer, all your makeup in one cosmetic case. Limit the number of shoes, socks, candles, chairs, sheets, pots, cutting boards, and collectibles you own. Limit your magazine subscriptions and the number of items on your coffee table. Limit your holiday decorations to one box and your sports equipment to one corner of the garage. Limit your plates, cups, and utensils to the size of your family and your garden supplies to the needs of your yard.

Back in the old days, Limits were applied by external factors: most significantly, the price and availability of material goods. Items were generally handmade and distributed locally–making them scarcer and more costly (relative to income) than in modern times. It was easy to be a minimalist a hundred years ago, as it was difficult enough to acquire the necessities–let alone anything extra. Nowadays, we can zip over to our local superstore and purchase whatever our heart desires; mass production and global distribution have made consumer items cheap, widely available, and easy to obtain. Sure, it's convenient, but as many of us have learned, it can be too much of a good thing. If we don't voluntarily limit our consumption, we can end up drowning in stuff!

Setting Limits not only helps *you,* it also eases other members of your household into a more minimalist lifestyle. Explain to your family that stuff must fit into the space allotted–and that when things overflow, they must be pared down. Limit your children's toys to one or two storage bins and your teenager's clothing to the size of her closet. They'll benefit enormously from this guidance and develop valuable habits for later in life. At the very least, limit each person's possessions to what fits into his or her room—be it a child's bedroom or playroom, or a spouse's office, craft room, or workshop. That way, you'll prevent personal stuff from spilling over into family space.

Of course, the ultimate limit on your possessions is set by the size of your house—which, as a minimalist, you may someday decide to reduce. Stuff expands to fill the space available (I'm pretty sure there's a physics equation for that). Limiting that space means less stuff, less clutter, less worries, and less stress. If you don't have a big house, you can't have a big houseful of stuff. Imagine moving from a studio apartment into a house with an attic, basement, and two-car garage—those storage spaces will undoubtedly fill up just because they're *there*. If you stopped using an exercise bike in your small apartment, you'd likely dispose of it, but in your bigger house, it would surely end up in the basement. Smaller digs put a natural limit on the number of things you can own—making it that much easier to live a minimalist lifestyle.

You may initially think that Limits will be stifling, but you'll soon discover that they're absolutely liberating! In a culture where we're conditioned to want more, buy more, and do more, they're a wonderful breath of relief. In fact, once you've discovered the joy of Limits, you'll be inspired to apply them to other parts of your life. Limiting commitments and activities can lead to a less harried lifestyle and free up valuable time. Limiting your spending slashes your credit card bills and boosts the balance in your bank account. Limiting processed, fatty, and sugary food can reduce your waistline and improve your health. The possibilities are, well . . . unlimited!

18
If one comes in, one goes out

Sometimes we declutter, and declutter, and declutter some more–but when we look at our homes, we don't see any progress. We can't understand it–we've filled up trash bags to put on the curb, we've filled up our trunks with stuff for charity, and we've filled up boxes to give to our brother-in-law. Yet it seems like we have just as much stuff in our closets, drawers, and basements. We're working hard, and we want to see results. What's the problem?

Think of your house and all the stuff in it as a bucket of water. Decluttering is like drilling a hole in the bottom–causing the bucket to empty slowly, drip by drip, as you rid your household of unwanted things. Great, that sounds like progress! As long as you keep up the good work, your stuff level should steadily decrease.

Here's the catch: the level only goes down if you stop pouring more in the top. Every item that enters your home is inflow into the bucket. So if you're still shopping, and buying things, and bringing home freebies from business conferences, those drips out the bottom won't do much good. The bucket will never empty, and may in fact overflow!

You can solve this problem by following a simple rule: If One Comes In, One Goes Out. Every time a new item comes into your home, a similar item must leave. For every drip into the bucket, there must be one drip out.

The One-In-One-Out rule is most effective when applied to like items. If a new shirt comes into the closet, an old shirt goes out. If a new book joins your collection, an old book leaves the shelf. If a new set of plates moves in, the old set of plates moves out. You can mix it up a little if you need to rebalance your possessions. For instance, if you have too many pants and too few shirts, ditch a pair of trousers when you buy a new top. Keep it equitable, though: tossing socks to offset a coat–or trading a paperclip for an office chair–doesn't fit the bill.

Too often, when we buy something new, we keep the item it's supposed to replace. Here's how it usually goes: we spy something in our house that's no longer up to snuff–perhaps it's out of style, falling apart, or just doesn't meet our needs. So we set out on a shopping mission, eager to ditch the old version in favor of a better, brighter, shinier, more technologically up-to-date one. We do our research, compare prices, read reviews, and finally make our purchase. Then something strange happens: when we bring home our new model, the old one doesn't look so forlorn. Although we'd deemed it not good enough to use, it still seems too good to throw away. We begin to imagine all the scenarios (however unlikely) in which we might need it. (As if we're expecting its brand-new, state-of-the-art replacement to up and stop working the following day.) Before we know it, the tired old thing is comfortably ensconced in our basement or attic, just in case it'll come in handy.

Every time a new item comes into your home, a similar item must leave.

The One-In-One-Out strategy helps you show your rejects the door—rather than house them in their retirement. As soon as that new model enters your home, bid your final farewell to the old. There's no magic to the system, but it does require discipline. I can tell you from experience that it's tempting to cheat and promise yourself you'll purge something later. You're so excited to wear that new sweater or use that new gadget that you don't feel like finding an appropriate swap. Nevertheless, summon up your minimalist powers, and commit to "one out" before you open, hang up, or use the "one in"–because unless you do it immediately, it'll likely never happen. I've gone so far as to keep new items, still packaged, in the trunk of my car until I was able to oust something old.

When you're starting to declutter, the One-In-One-Out rule is a wonderful stopgap measure. It caps your number of possessions and keeps you moving in the right direction. There's nothing more disheartening than working to purge ten items–agonizing over the decisions, summoning the strength to let them go–only to discover you accumulated twelve new ones in the meantime. Following this principle prevents such a scenario. From the second you commit to it, your household enters a steady state of stuff: as long as you stick with the program, you'll never own more than you do at that moment.

Better yet, as you continue to purge your possessions, you'll see a marked decrease in your stuff level. Since you've "shut off the tap," those drips out the bottom have a noticeable (and satisfying) effect. Of course, the more stuff you get rid of, the more rewarding the result, so in the next chapter, we'll turn the decluttering trickle into a steady flow.

19
Narrow down

In the previous chapter, we learned how to achieve a steady state of possessions by offsetting each item entering our home with a similar one leaving it. Fantastic! Now we no longer have to worry about taking one step forward and two steps back. With this system in place, each additional item we purge gets us that much closer to our minimalist goals.

To really make progress, though, we need to kick our decluttering efforts into high gear. Streamlining isn't about getting rid of a few things and then calling it done. Quite the contrary! It's designed to help us reach the holy grail of minimalist living: owning just enough to meet our needs–and nothing more. Therefore, when it comes to the stuff in our rooms, closets, and drawers, we have one mission: to Narrow Down.

Ideally, we want to reduce our possessions to the bare necessities. Now, before you get worried about having to live in a tent or sleep on the floor, let me explain. The bare necessities mean different things to different people. The minimalist residing on his sailboat may be able to meet his culinary needs with a single hot plate. Those of us with full kitchens, on the other hand, may consider our microwaves, pizza stones, and rice cookers indispensable. At the same time, the scuba gear he deems a necessity would likely be superfluous in our households.

Our personal essentials depend on a wide range of factors–like age, gender, occupation, hobbies, climate, culture, families, and peers. Minimalists in professional jobs may find business suits and dress shoes *de rigueur*, while those working from home can get by with smaller wardrobes. Parents with young children will have a different list of essentials than a bachelor living alone. Bookworms will have different necessities from sports enthusiasts; students will have different necessities from retirees; men will have different necessities from women.

Therefore, there's no master list of what's in a minimalist home. In fact, contrary to popular belief, there's not even a magic number. It doesn't matter if you own fifty, five hundred, or five thousand things–what matters is whether it's just enough (and not too much) for *you*. You must determine your own list of must-haves, then narrow your stuff down to match it.

This step, then, is about reducing our possessions to our personal "optimum" levels. Whenever we pick up an item, we should stop and think if we really need it—or can just as well get by without it. When we discover we have multiples, we should immediately cull the excess. When we unearth a box of unused stuff, we should seriously consider just dumping the lot. The good news: as we progress on our minimalist journeys, our number of "necessities" will slowly but surely decrease.

> You must determine your own list of must-haves, then narrow your stuff down to match it.

In addition to simply decluttering our stuff, we can also Narrow Down by more creative means—like choosing multi-functional items over single-use ones. A sleeper sofa eliminates the need for a separate guest bed. A printer with a scanner function means one less piece of office equipment. A smartphone can do the work of a calendar, wristwatch, calculator, appointment book, and more. Our goal is to accomplish the greatest number of tasks with the least number of items.

By the same token, we should favor versatile items over specialty ones. A large sauté pan can do the same job as a drawer full of specialty cookware. A classic black pump coordinates with both work and dress clothes, doing double duty in our wardrobe–as opposed to those fuchsia heels that hardly go with anything. An all-purpose cleaner can keep our homes sparkling, replacing separate sprays for the sink, tub, mirror, and countertops.

As we're happily Narrowing Down our items, however, some things will stop us in our tracks–and more often than not, they'll be sentimental in nature. Things with memories are just difficult to part with. But don't worry–we minimalists have ways of dealing with them, too. If you inherited a pile (or household) of a loved one's stuff, don't feel obligated to keep everything. One or two special pieces will preserve their memory just as well as the full lot. The same goes for boxes of school, wedding, baby, travel, you-name-it keepsakes. Select a single item to commemorate an event or experience. Take size and portability into consideration as well, and opt to cherish your grandfather's pocket watch over his grand piano.

Apply this same strategy to collections you inherit: rather than stash all twelve place settings of your grandmother's china in the attic, keep just a single plate and display it in a place of honor. Alternatively, take snapshots of the items and then declutter them; the photos preserve the memories without taking up the space. They're also more accessible–and easier to enjoy–than an item tucked away in storage.

Finally, we can Narrow Down our possessions by digitizing them. Entire collections of stuff–like music, movies, photos, video games, and books–can now be reduced to electronic bits and bytes. It's a wonderful time to be a minimalist.

If you embrace minimalism wholeheartedly, you'll find yourself continually on the lookout for new ways to Narrow Down your stuff. Be creative. Regard it as a personal challenge to do more with less, and have *fun* exploring all the possibilities. You may be surprised at what you can do without!

20
Everyday maintenance

Once we've worked through all the STREAMLINE steps–Starting over; separating our stuff into Trash, Treasure, and Transfer piles; making sure we have a good Reason for each item we own; finding a place for everything, and putting Everything in its place; keeping All our surfaces clear; arranging our things into Modules; imposing Limits on our possessions; heeding the "If one comes in, one goes out" rule; and Narrowing down our stuff–we can't simply call it a day and return to our old ways. Goodness no! We need to keep things up with some Everyday Maintenance.

Becoming a minimalist is a lifestyle change. We can't simply purge all our possessions in a no-holds-barred decluttering session, and then check it off as done. If so, we're likely to suffer a rebound effect and a new accumulation of clutter. Instead, we need to change our underlying attitudes (that's why we did all those mental exercises) and develop new habits (that's why we learned the STREAMLINE method). We must approach minimalist living not as a one-off activity, but as a wholesale lifestyle change.

Most important, we must continue to be vigilant about what enters our homes. Remember how we discussed being good gatekeepers? To maintain our minimalist lifestyles, we can never really let our guard down; things can get out of control quickly if we let them. Fortunately, the task is easier than it sounds, and soon becomes second nature. We simply have to establish routines to handle incoming stuff–like mail, catalogs, gifts, and freebies–and stick to them. Placing recycling and donation boxes near the front door, for example, works wonders–preventing tons of potential clutter with hardly any effort.

Yet sometimes it can feel like you're always on the defensive–trying single-handedly to stop the tsunami of stuff threatening your home. But you can play offense, too: by getting off mailing lists, canceling magazine subscriptions, opting out of gift exchanges, and generally making it known that you're pursuing a minimalist lifestyle. The last point is more important than you might think: because when they see your "empty" rooms, well-meaning friends and relatives may misinterpret your lack of stuff as a *need* for stuff. At best, you may be showered with unwanted gifts, and at worst, you may receive *their* cast-off clutter.

In addition to monitoring the front door, keep a sharp eye on clutter hotspots. As you know, clutter begets clutter. Once you let one item hang out for a while, it makes itself comfortable and invites over some friends. Don't let the party get started! It's a lot easier to kick out one unwelcome guest than a whole pack. In fact, if you don't act at the first signs of clutter, your radar becomes somewhat dulled. Think about it: there's a big difference between a perfectly clear surface and a surface with an item that doesn't belong. The wayward object sticks out like a sore thumb. However, the contrast between a surface with one wayward item versus one with two isn't quite so jarring–and even less so between one with two, and one with three (and so on). Best to clear off clutter as soon as you see it than risk a new accumulation.

The best part about minimalist living is that the rewards are immediate.

In the process, you'll often have to deal with other people's clutter. As you're generally not at liberty to dispose of it yourself, the best option is to return it post-haste to its rightful owner. If the items belong to a nonresident–like the stuff your sister stashed in your basement while moving (and still hasn't retrieved), or the craft project your friend abandoned on your dining room table–a quick phone call or email explaining your decluttering efforts should motivate them to collect their belongings.

More often, however, the wayward items belong to other household members. In that case, simply return them to the owner's personal space (like just inside their bedroom or office door). The idea is not to become everyone's maid, but to establish a boomerang effect–reinforcing the concept that anything that ventures into family space will be promptly returned. With any luck, they'll eventually get the picture and think twice before leaving things behind. Pointing out the offending clutter to its owner and giving them the choice of removal or disposal also does the trick quite nicely.

Finally, keep decluttering! The initial sweep through your house isn't the be-all and end-all of your purging; in fact, it's just the beginning. You'll find that your minimalist powers will grow stronger with time–and those must-haves that survived your first decluttering won't look as essential in the second round. For that reason, I recommend purging in cycles; after your initial decluttering, take another look around after a few weeks or months. You'll see your possessions with fresh eyes and a more seasoned perspective. In the meantime, you'll have started to experience the joy and freedom of a minimalist lifestyle–which will make you motivated (and excited) to dispose of more stuff. You'll be amazed how much easier it becomes to part with things in the second, third, fourth (or tenth or twentieth!) round.

Practice, of course, makes perfect. Therefore, instead of purging in spurts, you may prefer a slow and steady approach like the one-a-day declutter. Simply commit to disposing of one item each and every day. It can be anything: a worn-out pair of socks, a book you'll never read, a gift you could live without, a shirt that doesn't fit, or an outdated magazine. It takes little time or effort, and at the end of the year, your home will be 365 items lighter. To avoid putting useful items in a landfill, keep a donation box tucked away in your basement or hall closet. Add your discards one by one, and when it's full, donate it to Goodwill, the Salvation Army, or another charitable organization.

Alternatively, set decluttering goals for certain time periods: like ten items a week, or one hundred items a month. Keep a running tab of your castoffs to track your progress and maintain your motivation. Most important, have *fun* with it! The best part about minimalist living is that the rewards are immediate: every item you jettison instantly lightens your load. Do it daily, and you'll feel fantastic. You'll only regret that you didn't start sooner!

PART THREE

ROOM BY ROOM

Now for the exciting part: it's time to put our decluttering skills to work! In the following chapters, we'll apply the STREAMLINE method to specific rooms–learning how to Declutter, Contain, and Maintain the contents of each. Feel free to skip around, and start in any room you like. Begin with the easiest, the hardest, the smallest, the largest–whatever strikes your fancy. As you tackle each one in turn, space and serenity will spread throughout your home. So roll up your sleeves, and let the minimalist makeover begin!

21
Living or family room

In this chapter, we'll focus on the living room (or what you may call your family room). For our purposes, it's the area where family members congregate and guests hang out when they visit. In most homes, it's the largest space, and the one that sees the most action, so our decluttering efforts here will set a wonderful tone for the whole household.

Before we begin, however, I'd like you to leave your house. (Yes, you read that correctly.) Get up, walk out the door, and close it behind you. Once you're outside, clear your mind and enjoy the fresh air for a bit. By the time you return, I'll have decluttered your entire home with my magical minimalist superpowers! Just kidding, of course–but there is a point to this exercise.

Okay, you can go back inside now–but when you walk through the front door, *pretend you don't live there*. Enter as if you were a guest, with fresh eyes and an objective perspective.

So what's your first impression? Do you like what you see? Is your living room serene and inviting, welcoming you to stay? Or is it chaotic and cluttered, making you want to run away? More pointedly: if all this stuff weren't yours, would you have any desire to sit down and hang out in the middle of it?

We're taking a fresh look at our living rooms because clutter "disappears" when we grow accustomed to it. If the coffee table has been covered in magazines, knickknacks, craft supplies, and children's toys for weeks, months, or even years, we get used to it. We get used to the laundry basket in the corner, the books stacked next to the couch, and the DVDs piled around the TV. Somehow, the clutter becomes invisible to us.

After you've assessed the big picture, look closely at the room's contents. Scrutinize each piece of furniture, each throw pillow, and each tchotchke. Is every one of these items either useful or beautiful? Do they look harmonious with each other and appropriate in their places? Or does the scene resemble a flea market–or worse yet, the inside of a storage unit? If you emptied the contents onto your front lawn, would you bring it all back in–or would you be happy to evict a good portion?

DECLUTTER

Common advice says to start small and build up to larger tasks. Not a bad idea, but let's do something different here–let's do something BIG. Your living room houses some substantial items and offers a great opportunity to start with a bang. Purging just one piece of unnecessary (or unloved) furniture can make a dramatic impact–and provide wonderful incentive to slog through smaller items. It's like that worn-out chair or orphan end table is a giant plug in your stopped-up sink of stuff; once you yank it out, it clears the way for a gush of clutter.

So focus first on your big stuff. Is every piece of furniture used regularly, or are some items there for no better reason than "they always have been"? Consider how you and your family use the room. Do you congregate on the couch or the floor? Does anyone ever sit in the corner chair? Would you have more room for activities (lounging, playing games, gathering for a movie) if you had fewer pieces of furniture?

If you target a major item you'd like to toss–but still feel a little hesitant–move it out of the room for a few days.

By all means, don't feel obligated to own certain items simply because they're expected (as in, "My goodness, what would the neighbors think if we didn't have a recliner?").

When my husband and I lived overseas, we decided we didn't need a couch. Although we'd never seen a home without one, it simply didn't suit our lifestyle (we had neither a TV, nor frequent visitors, and spent our evenings and weekends out on the town). Therefore, we furnished our living room with just two lounge chairs and a coffee table. Those three pieces were enough to meet our needs; anything more would have been too much.

If you target a major item you'd like to toss–but still feel a little hesitant–move it out of the room for a few days. Temporarily stow it in the basement or attic, and note if anyone misses it. Sometimes simply moving a piece out of the way gives you a better perspective on it, and once it has left its spot, it's easier to sever ties with it.

After you've dealt with the large items, it's time to move on to the smaller ones–and depending on your living room, there may be quite a few. Don't panic; this is where we'll break things up into smaller, more manageable tasks. The best way to tackle it: go shelf by shelf, drawer by drawer, pile by pile. Simply clear off the contents (or dump them out), and sort them into your Trash, Treasure, and Transfer piles. Most important, don't rush through it. Take the time to do a thorough job–even if it takes weeks or months to sort through every last drawer. Such attentiveness will bring far greater rewards in the long run.

Try clearing the room entirely of decorative, nonfunctional pieces–sweep them from the shelves, the mantel, the console, and the side tables. Store them away in a box, and live without them for a week. Sometimes extraneous items can stifle our enjoyment of a space without us even realizing it. When they're gone, we feel a wave of relief–like we finally have the room to stretch out and move around (without hitting or breaking anything). Notice how family members and guests react to the decluttered space–are they more relaxed? Do they move around more freely? Are they more enthusiastic to engage in activities?

Let's consider some more ways we can Narrow Down here. Ideally, we want nothing more than that which meets our needs. At the bare minimum, a living room needs some sort of seating for household members. Extreme minimalists (and those of non-Western cultures) may be perfectly content with a few floor cushions. A bachelor may get by with a lounge chair. A family, on the other hand, may deem a sofa a necessity. Ask yourself–if you only have three people in your household, do you really need furniture that seats eight? You can always rustle up some folding chairs if you have guests (or create a fun, bohemian atmosphere by lounging on the floor). Consider the footprint of the furniture, too; I've seen overstuffed, oversized sectionals that nearly filled the entire room. Is the "comfort" of such a behemoth really worth the floor space it devours? Could you meet your seating needs with something smaller and slimmer?

Next, let's talk tables. Again, most living rooms will require at least one table to accommodate the family's activities. A small coffee table may be perfectly adequate. If the room also serves as an office or craft space, an additional desk or work-table may be needed. Anything beyond that, however, is often merely decorative. Think long and hard about whether you really need the end tables, side tables, and console tables that currently dwell in the room.

Another way to minimize is to invest in multi-functional furniture. As mentioned earlier, a sleeper sofa can serve as both your family's couch and guest bed. A coffee table with built-in drawers or cabinets can eliminate the need for other storage pieces and free up significant floor space. The same goes for ottomans: if you're going to have one, make it do double-duty and stash some of your stuff. Such pieces provide maximum functionality with a minimum footprint, leaving us much more room to move around.

Your living room might also contain an entertainment center for the television and electronics. But ask yourself this: do you really need the TV? Shocking as it may seem, plenty of people (my family included) live perfectly fulfilling, entertaining, and informed lives without one. Plus, you can stream just about anything these days on your laptop or computer. The bonus: when you don't have a TV, you don't need a cabinet, stand, or any other piece of furniture to hold it. (Alternatively, you can save space–and still keep the TV–by mounting it on the wall.)

Most of our living rooms also have some sort of shelving, usually crammed with stuff. All I can say is that the less stuff you have, the less shelving you need–so get to work culling those collections! Cultivate hobbies that require little in terms of supplies, like singing, origami, or learning a new language; and play games that involve a small deck of cards, instead of large boards and hundreds of plastic pieces. Use creative strategies to meet your entertainment needs–like borrowing items from friends or the library instead of owning them.

For those titles you *do* wish to own, consider going digital. Download movies, convert your music, and invest in an electronic reader–a single device can hold hundreds of ebooks (and give you access to thousands of others), eliminating the need for entire bookshelves. Only buy print titles that you know you will cherish. Store all your photos digitally, printing only those you want to give as gifts or display in your home.

CONTAIN

Since the living room sees so much action, it's particularly important that everything has a place. Otherwise, things can become truly chaotic!

Define the regions where you watch TV, store movies, read magazines, play games, and use the computer. Make sure that the objects involved with said activities are housed in their appropriate area, and do everything you can to prevent them from straying into another. Magazines shouldn't be stacked on the television, and playthings shouldn't reside on the couch. Involve all household members in the process so that everyone will understand the system and share responsibility for maintaining it.

The less stuff you have, the less shelving you need–so get to work culling those collections!

If the living room also functions as someone's office or craft space, restrict the activity (and its accessories) to a well-defined area. If it helps, use a standing screen or floor plant to create a visual (and psychological) boundary. The reason is two-fold: first, you want to keep the office supplies from spilling over into the main living space. Second, you want to keep the office area free of clutter and distraction–you'll be much more productive when you don't have to clear toys from your desk before using it.

Assign your stuff to your Inner Circle, Outer Circle, and Deep Storage. As you recall, your Inner Circle items are those you use on a regular (daily, or almost daily) basis. They should be kept in easy-to-access locations, such as mid-level shelves and drawers. Candidates for your living room's Inner Circle include the remote control, current magazines, frequently used electronics and computer peripherals, and favorite books, movies, and games. Your Outer Circle should house items used less than once a week, like certain hobby and craft supplies, reference books, and items for entertaining guests. Store these on upper and lower shelves, and in less accessible drawers and cabinets. Seasonal decorations, and pieces you treasure but can't currently display (in an effort, perhaps, to toddler-proof the room) belong in Deep Storage–preferably in the basement, attic, or other out-of-the-way place.

Next create Modules for your various collections–like video games, books, magazines, and electronics. Instead of storing them in a jumbled mess, separate them from each other and designate a specific shelf, drawer, or container for each category. Consolidating like items helps us easily spot duplicates, weed out undesirables, and grasp the size of our collections. It also helps us and other family members return things to their dedicated spots–preventing them from drifting throughout the room or straying into other parts of the house.

Modules are particularly useful for organizing craft and hobby supplies. Instead of housing them in a common drawer or cabinet, separate the materials by activity: knitting, scrapbooking, painting, model building, jewelry making, et cetera. Assign each activity its own container: clear plastic storage bins work well, as do the heavy cardboard boxes in which reams of paper are sold. Deep, rectangular baskets will also do the trick. When you're ready to engage in a particular hobby, simply retrieve its Module and unpack its supplies. When you're finished, cleanup is a cinch: put everything back into the container, and return it to its proper storage space.

As minimalists, we want to Limit our collections to our favorite items; otherwise, they tend to grow unchecked, and before we know it, we're inundated with stuff. The Limits can be defined as either a certain number or a certain amount of space. When dealing with books, for example, you may decide to cap your collection at one hundred or with the available space on your bookshelf. Either way, you're putting a lid on the total amount and ensuring that your library contains only your most loved and most frequently read volumes.

In your living room, put Limits on every type of possession that resides there. Once you've reached them, purge the old before adding something new. Our tastes change over the years; we grow tired of the movies, music, and pastimes we once loved. Instead of retaining them indefinitely, periodically cull through them and donate the ones you no longer enjoy. A fresh, pared-down collection is much more pleasant to browse than an indiscriminate hodgepodge of titles. If you crave novelty, borrow from the library instead of buying; that way, you can enjoy a wide variety of entertainment without the headache (or expense) of ownership.

Take inspiration from traditional Japanese homes, in which only one or two carefully chosen pieces are displayed at a time.

In the case of hobby and craft supplies, your Modules provide a natural limit on the amount of materials you keep on hand. If they're reaching full capacity, refrain from further accumulation until you've winnowed down your current supply–either by tackling planned projects, completing unfinished ones, or simply clearing out what you don't intend to use. Imposing Limits gives you the perfect excuse to purge unwanted materials (like the chartreuse yarn, chintzy beads, or cheap fabric)–the mere sight of which can dampen your enthusiasm for the activity in question. Pick your favorites and pitch the rest!

Limit your collectibles as well. I don't know if the drive to collect is inherent in human nature, but at some point in our lives, most of us have accumulated certain things simply for the sake of it: be it baseball cards, vintage teacups, first edition books, movie memorabilia, commemorative coins, foreign stamps, or antique nutcrackers. We enjoy the thrill of the hunt and the excitement of finding a new item (the rarer, the better) to add to our collection.

Unfortunately, however, the Internet (and eBay in particular) has made tracking down such "treasures" far too easy. In the past, our collections were curbed by limited availability and access; we actually had to scour antique stores and flea markets for new finds. Now a world of stuff is at our fingertips; in a few hours online, we can acquire a collection that formerly took years to build. Therefore, we must impose our *own* Limits on collectibles–restricting our acquisitions to a fixed number instead of purchasing everything we can find.

Finally, set Limits on your decorative items. Take inspiration from traditional Japanese homes, in which only one or two carefully chosen pieces are displayed at a time. In this way, you can honor and appreciate those items that are most meaningful to you–instead of making them compete for attention with a dozen others. That doesn't mean you have to toss the rest of your décor (unless, of course, you want to). Simply create a décor Module to store your favorite pieces; bring them out for display a few at a time, and rotate them throughout the year.

The One-In-One-Out rule helps further contain our living room stuff by making sure nothing *more* comes in. If we bring home a new book or game, an old one must leave. When the latest issue of a magazine arrives, toss the old one in the recycling bin (or pass it on to friends or relatives). If you start a new hobby, give up a former one that no longer excites you–along with all the supplies. If you're out shopping and a piece of décor catches your fancy, determine what you'll give up before bringing it home (if it doesn't merit the sacrifice, skip it and wait for something better). Make this a habit, and it'll transform your living room: instead of being a stale memorial to old interests and pastimes, it'll be a dynamic space reflecting your family's current tastes.

MAINTAIN

If a neighbor dropped by at this very moment, could you set refreshments on the coffee table? If your kids wanted to play a game or work on an art project, is there any place to do so? Or would either scenario be delayed (or forsaken) because you have to clear off too much stuff? If you felt inspired to do a little yoga, is there ample room on the floor–or would you get more of a workout moving around furniture and other contents to make some space?

Our living rooms are for living. If we treat them as makeshift storage units, we're destroying the functionality of the room–and cheating ourselves (and our families) out of very valuable space. The surfaces in particular–like the coffee table, side tables, worktable, or desk–are of supreme importance.

If they're haphazardly piled with magazines, junk mail, toys, books, and unfinished craft projects, they're useless for our current activities. Likewise, family room surfaces shouldn't be reserved for a lifeless parade of ceramic figurines–quite the opposite. They're meant for four-year-olds to color, teenagers to play games with their friends, and adults to enjoy a cup of coffee.

We should keep the floor (our largest surface) as clear as possible, too. Children in particular need space to roam, frolic, and explore; they shouldn't be cramped into a tiny play area, barely visible among wall-to-wall furniture and mountains of clutter. Adults also benefit from a serene, uncluttered space. When we come home after a long workday, we need room to unwind, both mentally and physically. If we're tripping over objects on the way to the couch, or looking around at a jumble of stuff, we feel stressed, stifled, and irritated. By contrast, when the room is spare and tidy, we have plenty of space–and peace of mind–to kick back, relax, and breathe.

To borrow a term from the corporate world, we should think of our living rooms as "flex space." In an office, flex space is a work area open for anyone's use. When an employee arrives in the morning, he sets up at an available (empty) desk for the day. When he leaves in the evening, he takes all his belongings with him, leaving the desk free and clear for someone else to use the following day. Our living rooms should function similarly: the floor and surfaces should stand empty, ready to accommodate the day's activities; when those activities cease, they should be cleared of all items, leaving them open and available for the next person to use.

> We should think of our living rooms as "flex space."

Furthermore, we must always keep our defense shields at the ready. This room is only steps from the front door and is often the first place incoming objects come to rest. (In fact, some of them seem to get stuck here forever.) Patrol the area for intruders. (What's in that box by the door? Whose jacket is draped over the couch? Is that junk mail on the coffee table?) When you spot stuff that doesn't belong, don't throw up your hands in exasperation–fight back. Flush out those invaders at first sight, and make sure that anything entering or traveling through the room doesn't get a chance to stop. Hang up coats, put away shoes, handle the mail, and take new purchases directly to their appropriate spots.

Keep a close eye on where clutter tends to gather–such as the coffee table, end table, or any other surfaces in the room. If you straighten up after each and every activity, the clutter has no chance to accumulate. Furthermore, if you discover wayward items while vacuuming or dusting, don't clean around them–clean them up!

To complicate matters, the living room is where you'll most often encounter other people's clutter. Ideally, this problem will wane with time, as household members learn to respect the flex space and take personal items with them when they leave the room. In the meantime, however, you may have to take control and boomerang that stuff right back to its owners. Get in the habit of doing a clean sweep of the space each evening before bed and clearing it of stuff that doesn't belong. It takes just a few minutes but makes a huge difference. You can nag, and preach, and talk about keeping things tidy all day–but the best way to inspire others is to lead by example.

22 Bedroom

The bedroom, more than anywhere else in the house, should be a place of peace and serenity, a haven from our hectic lives. Therefore, we have some important work ahead–but after we're through, we'll have the perfect environment for a well-deserved rest.

Your bedroom should be the most uncluttered room in your house. It serves an incredibly important function: providing solace for your weary soul after a hard day of work, school, childcare, housecleaning, and every other activity you manage to fit into your day. It should be a place of rest and relaxation–not only for your body, but also for your mind.

Take a few moments, close your eyes, and envision your ideal bedroom. Picture every detail, as if it were a magazine layout: the style of bed; the color of the sheets, duvet, and blanket; the pillows, the lighting, the flooring, the décor, and the other furnishings in the room. What kind of mood does it have–calm, romantic, luxurious? Although I don't know your personal tastes, I'm pretty sure of one thing: there's not a stitch of clutter in your dream room. And rightly so–it's hard to feel pampered when you're buried in stuff.

To Start Over, then, move everything out of the room except the bed. Since the room by definition is for sleeping (and we don't want to throw out our backs), this piece of furniture can stay. Likewise, leave in place any large, wardrobe-related items that you'll definitely keep, like an armoire or dresser. But for now, everything else goes: desks, tables, chairs, storage boxes, laundry bins, potted plants, treadmills, ab crunchers, televisions, computers, lamps, books, magazines, vases, knickknacks, and so forth. Empty it down to its bare bones, and put everything in an adjacent room for the time being.

Now lie down on the bed and look around. Quite a change, isn't it? You probably never realized how much space you actually have. Does it feel more open, peaceful, and relaxing? Is it easier to stretch out, clear your mind, and breathe? That's how a bedroom *should* feel! It should refresh and rejuvenate you, not make you stressed out and tired. The best part: creating this idyllic atmosphere doesn't require an interior decorator or expensive renovation. All you have to do is declutter!

DECLUTTER

Make your Trash, Treasure, and Transfer piles, and start sorting through your bedroom's contents. Don't bother with clothing or accessories just yet; that's a job unto itself, and we'll tackle it in the next chapter. For now, concentrate on everything else–particularly those items that have nothing to do with sleeping or dressing.

> The main function of our bedrooms is to provide space for sleeping and clothes storage.

You'll likely encounter an interesting dilemma here: you'll find items that aren't appropriate for *any* of those piles. You don't want to dispose of them in the Trash pile or put them in the Transfer pile to sell or give away; in fact, you'd really like to keep them. However, they can't go in your bedroom's Treasure pile, because they aren't related to sleep or clothing. The problem: the items may belong in your life, but they don't belong in the bedroom.

Unfortunately, our bedrooms tend to function as overflow drains for our stuff; when our living areas get too full, the spillover leaks through our bedroom doors. Imagine you're expecting guests in an hour and are frantically picking up the living and dining rooms. You've shoved what you can in the closets and drawers, but inevitably run out of space. So what do you do? Stash the excess in the bedroom. At least you can shut the door and hide it from sight while entertaining. All too often, though, that refugee stuff gains asylum there–and before long, you're using your bedroom as an ad hoc solution to your clutter problem.

Feel free, then, to redefine your Transfer pile to "Transfer Out of the Room," and include in it any object that belongs elsewhere in the house. This pile might contain anything from magazines to your children's toys to your rowing machine. You may even decide to add some keepsakes and sentimental items to the mix. Make sure, however, that these items have a rightful place *somewhere*. The last thing you want to do is shuffle a pile of homeless junk from room to room. If an item's function is so vague that you don't know where to put it, the best place for it may be in your donation box.

The main function of our bedrooms is to provide space for sleeping and clothes storage. Therefore, when we ask the resident items their raison d'être, the answer better have something to do with rest, relaxation, or wardrobe–otherwise, they may face deportation.

Your bed's probably feeling pretty smug right now, knowing it'll pass this test with flying colors. The objects on your nightstand, vanity, or dresser may be a little more nervous–but some of them actually have every right to be there. The alarm clock is safe, as are your glasses, tissues, and the book you're currently reading. You might keep that vase of flowers, and a few candles–they certainly help create a romantic or relaxing atmosphere. A handful of other objects may also gain access to this coveted, cozy space–but to be honest, I can't think of too many. "Because there's nowhere else to put them" is *not* a good reason to keep them here.

Now let's discuss those things that don't belong here but often try to muscle their way in. That pesky laundry basket, for example; sure, the bed provides an excellent surface for folding clothes–but do it and be done with it already! Piles of socks and t-shirts aren't exactly conducive to a romantic evening. The same goes for your toddler's toys; it's hard to heat things up next to a herd of stuffed animals.

Craft supplies are another issue. They often migrate to this room when they can't find shelter elsewhere. But unless you're knitting in your sleep, yarn and needles should be banished from the bedroom. If it's a pre-bedtime activity, we'll make an exception; in that case, stash the stuff in a box or bag and slip it under the bed. By the same token, find somewhere else to store exercise equipment and computer supplies; hard drives and hand weights are hardly soothing.

Perhaps I don't give a fair shake to knickknacks, but I think they have little place in the bedroom. A few special pieces are acceptable, but do question whether you need fifteen of them lined up across your dresser. The more stuff on your surfaces, the harder they are to clean–and who wants to spend *any* extra time on housework?

Now let's see how else we can Narrow Down–in my opinion, this is where the real minimalist fun begins! I've always had somewhat of a rebellious streak, and breaking the rules of consumer (or decorative) propriety is my little way of sticking it to the man. Nowhere is this more fun, or socially acceptable, than in the bedroom!

Our bedrooms are our own little worlds. Few outsiders enter this intimate space, and those that do know us pretty well (and presumably won't judge us by our lack of furnishings). Therefore, we can feel free to explore our minimalist fantasies here without regard for social norms. That sounds fun, doesn't it? In your living room, it may be awkward to seat guests on the floor, but in your bedroom, nobody knows (or cares) if you're sleeping on it.

As a child, I had a well-appointed little princess's room: a beautiful canopy bed, floral duvet and curtains, and entire suite of vanity, dressers, and bookcases. Almost every inch of floor space was occupied by a piece of furniture, save a few feet on each side of the bed. Though it was very pretty, I found it suffocating; I never felt like I had enough room to stretch out my young limbs and move around freely. As a teenager, however, I cajoled my parents into letting me "redecorate." Out went the dressers, vanity, and nightstands, and I traded the fancy bed for a mattress and box spring on a simple frame. My bedroom went from 80 percent furniture, 20 percent floor space to the opposite–and I loved the transformation. (Thus, a minimalist was born!)

Today, my husband and I have nothing in our bedroom save a futon mattress on the floor. That may not work for everyone, but it works for us. By eliminating the bed frame, we also eliminated the need for nightstands. Instead of using dressers, we store all clothing in our closets, organized with hanging fabric shelving and a handful of containers. We don't have a vanity, preferring to perform all grooming in the bathroom. Keeping things to the bare minimum gives our bedroom an open, airy, spacious feel–exactly what we need after a busy day in a crowded world.

The point I want to emphasize is that you don't have to own certain pieces of furniture simply because it's expected. Just because a bedroom set has six matching pieces doesn't mean you have to buy (or keep) all of them. Not everyone needs a vanity; not everyone needs a dresser; not everyone needs a nightstand. Heck, not everyone needs a bed! Forget what all the design magazines tell you about how a master bedroom should look. Instead, stop and contemplate what *you* really need. Narrow Down the pieces in your bedroom to a functional minimum, and reclaim all that glorious space–the neighbors never have to know that you live without a nightstand.

Seek ways to minimize your linens as well. Question whether it's necessary to have separate winter and summer bedding; in most climates, simple cotton will suffice year round. By the same token, choose a duvet (and cover) that'll work in every season. Instead of stockpiling sheets for an army, pare down your collection to the essential. By making wise choices, you can reduce the contents of your linen closet without sacrificing comfort.

You don't have to own certain pieces of furniture simply because it's expected.

CONTAIN

For our bedrooms to be peaceful and serene, everything in them must have a place. When stuff is tucked away, a sense of calm prevails; stray items, on the other hand, disturb our restful ambience.

The Inner Circle of your bedroom should contain those items in daily use: like an alarm clock, reading glasses, grooming items, and in-season clothing. Of course, these things should all be in their appropriate places rather than strewn about the room. Clothes should be in the closet and dressers–*not* piled on the floor or draped over chairs. Make it a habit to fold, hang up, or toss your clothing in the hamper immediately upon removal. Corral cosmetics in a makeup bag or container, and ensure that all accessories–like shoes, belts, handbags, and jewelry–have designated spots in your closet or drawers. The stuff of your Inner Circle should be within reach, though not necessarily within sight.

Reserve your Outer Circle for things like extra linens and out-of-season clothing. As for Deep Storage, I can't think of a single bedroom item that would be suitable. Garages, attics, and basements aren't optimal places for storing bedding, and furthermore, any bedding you own should be in regular rotation in your household.

If you don't have a linen closet elsewhere in the house, use Modules in the bedroom for your extra bedding. Plastic, under-the-bed containers are perfect for storing additional sheets, pillowcases, and blankets. Do the same for each bedroom in your house, so everyone has immediate and easy access to their own linens. That way, you'll avoid the mess that can result when they're all piled together on a shelf.

When you consolidate your linens, you might be surprised at how many you have. Sheets and blankets seem to multiply when we're not looking. Every so often, we buy a new set–because we want a fresh look, our old ones are getting shabby, or guests are on the way–with little thought to those we already own. The old ones get relegated to a "just in case" pile, and our collection grows with each passing year. Putting them into Modules provides a wonderful opportunity to cull them to a reasonable amount.

Take it a step further and Limit your linens to a certain number. Two sets of sheets per bed are generally sufficient, and can be rotated with your laundry schedule. In the case of blankets and quilts, climate also plays a role; the warmer your region, the fewer you'll need. In general, don't keep more linens than your family (and guests) can reasonably use at any given time. Stick to the One-In-One-Out rule, and the next time you acquire new bedding, donate the old–and think of the warmth and comfort you're so generously providing someone else.

If you keep grooming items in the bedroom, make Modules for them as well. Store cosmetics, combs, hairbrushes, and styling products in a small bag or container that can be tucked away when not in use. Why display your entire arsenal of beauty items for your partner (or overnight guests) to see? Better to maintain a little mystery than ruin a romantic atmosphere with a lineup of hairspray, foot powder, or deodorant on your dresser. You may also want to assign a small tray, box, or designated drawer for the stuff that comes out of your pockets each day–like your wallet, loose change, transit cards, and keys. Consolidating them looks neater and makes them much easier to find the next morning.

MAINTAIN

Now let's talk about the most important surface in this room: the bed. It should always be clear–no ifs, ands, or buts about it. Your bed is essential to your health and well-being and is used at least a quarter of every day; therefore, it should always stand ready to serve its intended purpose.

Your bed is a functional surface, not a decorative one–so keep the fancy throw pillows and other nonessentials to a minimum. It's a drag to clear off the bed each night before climbing into it, and the less stuff you have to straighten and arrange, the better. Take a cue from luxury hotels and keep it simple: crisp white sheets and pillowcases topped with a fluffy duvet make for a heavenly, minimalist retreat. Just note that when I say the bed is a functional surface, I don't mean it should serve every function imaginable; it's not meant to be your laundry station, workspace, or play area for your kids. If it happens to serve one of these purposes temporarily, remove the clothes, paperwork, or children's toys immediately thereafter.

Of course, the bed isn't the only surface that requires monitoring. The more pieces of furniture you have–nightstands, vanities, dressers, tables–the more vigilant you need to be (a great reason for having less furniture!). Don't let these pieces gather wayward items. Clear off their tops and reserve them for the handful of things that truly belong there. Last but not least, don't forget about the floor. Banish those stacks of books and magazines (how many can you read at a time, anyway?), and anything else that may have accumulated while you weren't paying attention. Above all, don't let any clothing get underfoot and lay the foundation for a pile. Once you start a "floordrobe," you have a much larger problem; a growing mountain of apparel isn't good for your ambience or your clothes. In fact, the only part of the floor that's fair game for stuff is under the bed. Use–but don't abuse–everyone's favorite storage space; in other words, don't make it a hiding place for clutter.

The bedroom may not see the same traffic as other parts of the house; however, it still needs daily maintenance to keep it clean and clutter-free.

Number one on the agenda: make the bed every day. This simple action takes just a few minutes, but it can completely transform the room. A made bed is one of life's little luxuries, inviting you to slip in and relax after a hard day's work. It exudes calm and is a powerful influence in keeping the bedroom neat and tidy. When the bed is undone, a mess in the rest of the room doesn't seem out of place; everything just looks a wreck. In contrast, when your bedding is smoothed, tucked, and folded just so, the clutter has no camouflage and is much less likely to accumulate.

Keep it simple: crisp white sheets and pillowcases topped with a fluffy duvet make for a heavenly, minimalist retreat.

Number two: scan the room for wayward clothes. Sometimes when we take off a jacket, sweater, or pair of stockings—especially if we're falling into bed after a long day—the item fails to reach its appropriate spot. As soon as you notice such a stray article, put it away. It can be particularly hard to corral shoes and handbags; these items like to go out on the town, and you'll often find a crowd of them waiting at the door. Give them their own special space in the closet (to which they're returned each night), so they don't take up space in *your* part of the room.

Third, monitor the bedroom for uninvited "guests." As private a space as it is, some things still manage to sneak in (usually in the arms of other family members). If you catch your toddler's stuffed toy or spouse's tennis racket lurking in the corner, don't invite it to stay the night—boomerang it right back where it belongs. Similarly, when you're finished reading that mystery novel, don't let it take up residence by your bedside. Unless you keep a bookshelf in your bedroom, return it to its appropriate Module in the living room or office. Clear the room before you close your eyes, and you'll wake up to a wonderful, serene space each morning!

23
Wardrobe

It's time to tackle the clutter in our closets. If you have plenty of clothes but nothing to wear, this chapter's for you. We'll explore how paring down our attire can save us time, money, space, and stress–while making it *easier* for us to look well-dressed. Having a streamlined wardrobe is one of the true joys of being a minimalist!

Cleaning out your closet doesn't have to be a chore; on the contrary, it can be a blast! In fact, it's one of my favorite decluttering activities. The task is certainly easier than tackling an entire room: there's no furniture to worry about, tchotchkes to deliberate over, or other people's stuff to deal with. To be honest, I think of it more as "me time" than cleaning time. I like to put on some music, have a glass of wine, and stage my own fashion show as I rummage through my wardrobe. Purging dowdy old things and planning fabulous new outfits makes for a fun couple of hours, and having extra closet space in the end is a wonderful reward.

To Start Over, take everything out of your closet, dressers, and armoire, and lay it on your bed. And by everything, I mean *everything*! Reach into those dark recesses and pull out the bell-bottoms, bubble skirt, and bridesmaid dress from your sister's wedding. Fish out those cowboy boots, platform sandals, and strappy stilettos you've never been able to walk in. Dump all the underwear, socks, pajamas, and pantyhose out of their respective drawers, and line up your handbags for inspection. Keep going until you're left with empty drawers, bare shelves, and naked hangers.

But before we continue, let's stop for some soul-searching. To create a minimalist wardrobe, we need to know what's *right* for us. Spend some time pondering your personal style: is it classic, sporty, preppy, punk, bohemian, glamorous, vintage, romantic, or modern? Do you prefer pastels, jewel tones, or bold primaries? Do you look best in clothes that are closely tailored or loose and flowing? What fabrics make you feel most comfortable? Keep your answers in mind as you evaluate your clothing. Pieces that don't fit your style or preferences are likely to spend more time in your closet than on your body.

Next, imagine that a fire, flood, or other disaster has wiped out your entire wardrobe, and you must rebuild from scratch. Your funds are limited, so you have to make smart choices.

Consider the absolute essentials you would need for a typical week. Your list might include socks, underwear, one or two pairs of pants, a couple of shirts, a jacket, a versatile pair of shoes, and perhaps a sweater, skirt, and pair of pantyhose or tights (forget the last two if you're a guy). You'll want to choose items that are appropriate for both work and weekend, and can be layered to keep you comfortable in a range of temperatures. You'll need to be able to mix and match them and create a variety of outfits from just a few pieces. This exercise illuminates your most functional articles of clothing and lays a good foundation for your minimalist wardrobe.

DECLUTTER

Now that everything's out of your closet, try everything on. If you haven't worn that party dress or three-piece suit in five years, how do you know it still fits? Don each item in turn, and do a three-sixty or two in front of the mirror. We all know that just because something looks good on a hanger doesn't mean it looks good on us; and conversely, an item that's ho-hum on its own may come alive when we put it on.

Make your Trash, Treasure, and Transfer piles, and psych yourself up for some serious decision-making. Use boxes or garbage bags for your castoffs–not to throw them away, but to keep them out of sight. It'll reduce the temptation to retrieve things from the reject pile. If your resolve starts to waver, take a break and re-read the philosophy chapters in Part One. Sometimes all you need is a little pep talk to keep you going!

In your Trash pile, put all those items that are beyond repair (or your ability or desire to do so)–like that holey sweater or shirt with a stubborn stain. If you can't reach into your closet, put it on, and wear it in public, it doesn't belong there. That doesn't mean they're destined for the landfill. If you can recycle or repurpose them, all the better–but only keep them if you have a specific use in mind.

The number one reason to keep an article of clothing is that *you wear it.*

If we only had to deal with worn-out items, decluttering would be a snap! However, most of our clothes wear out their welcome long before they wear out. Put in your Transfer pile any items that make you feel self-conscious, uncomfortable, or unfashionable–in other words, all those perfectly good clothes that are no longer good for you. Instead of letting them languish in your closet, give them a chance at a second life. If an item still has its tags, try to return it–most retailers will accept unworn clothing for thirty to ninety days after purchase. Otherwise, sell it online or in a consignment shop, or donate it to a charitable organization.

Work through the STREAMLINE method to find your Treasures, and you'll soon have a minimalist wardrobe. But if you prefer to proceed more slowly, here's an alternative technique that takes little effort. Obtain three spools of ribbon in green, yellow, and red. After you wear an item, tie the hanger with a bow: green if it made you feel fabulous, red if it made you feel frumpy, or yellow if you're on the fence about it. At the end of six months, keep the greens and yellows as your Treasures, and Trash or Transfer the reds. If something doesn't have a ribbon, it means you haven't worn it at all–and you know exactly where that belongs!

The number one reason to keep an article of clothing is that *you wear it*. Well, that should be easy, right? Wouldn't that justify the majority of our apparel? Not so fast. According to the Pareto principle, or 80/20 rule, we wear 20 percent of our wardrobe 80 percent of the time. Uh-oh! That means we *don't wear* the majority of our clothing–at least not often. We could pare down our wardrobes to one-fifth their size, and hardly miss a thing.

Clothing *that fits you* has good reason to stay in your closet. Conversely, if it doesn't fit, you can't wear it, and if you can't wear it, why keep it? Don't store different clothes for different weights; reward yourself with a new wardrobe *after* you drop those pounds. (What great incentive to skip dessert and hit the gym!)

Items *that flatter you* are also welcome in your wardrobe. Decide which sleeve length makes your arms look sexy, and which skirt length best shows off your legs. Determine which colors complement your skin tone, and which ones wash you out. Base your wardrobe on your body, not on trends. When considering an outfit, question whether you'd feel comfortable being photographed or running into your ex while wearing it. If the answer is "no," out it goes.

Clothes that *suit your lifestyle* are also keepers. List the activities for which you need apparel–such as work, social functions, gardening, leisure, and exercise–and evaluate your pieces accordingly. Resist the temptation to hold on to "fantasy" clothes; a closet full of cocktail dresses won't make you a socialite. Devote your space to what you'll wear in real life instead. Adjust your wardrobe to accommodate life changes: banish those business suits if you now work at home, or shed that sheepskin coat if you've moved to a warmer climate.

Don't save something simply because you paid good money for it. I know it's hard to toss that cashmere sweater or those designer heels, even if you never wear them–if they're still in your closet, you feel you haven't wasted your money (been there, done that). But you're better off selling them to recoup some cash, or donating them to charity. In the latter case, the money "spent" will at least go to a good cause.

In essence, a minimalist wardrobe is what is popularly known as a capsule wardrobe: a small set of essential pieces that can be mixed and matched into a variety of outfits. First, select a base color–such as black, brown, gray, navy, cream, or khaki–and limit foundation pieces (like pants and skirts) to that shade. I chose black–mainly because it's flattering on me, travels well, and hides stains–and purged all my navies, browns, and tans in the process. Not only did this strategy slash the size of my wardrobe, it helped me vastly reduce my accessories. I was thrilled to find I no longer needed footwear and handbags in multiple colors. A black purse or pair of shoes goes with everything in my closet–which means I can get by with far fewer of them.

Ideally, you should be able to get dressed in the dark and still look fabulous.

Don't worry, this strategy doesn't mean you have to dress in monochrome–now you get to choose accent colors. Select a handful of shades that flatter you and work well with your neutral (I chose burgundy, plum, aqua, and teal). Stick to these colors when selecting shirts, sweaters, and other pieces to supplement your basics. For variety, you can add a secondary neutral: I have skirts and pants in gray as well as black. You might choose khaki in addition to brown, or cream in addition to navy–just make sure all your colors can be mixed and matched. Ideally, you should be able to get dressed in the dark and still look fabulous.

Next, focus on versatility. Any candidate for your capsule must be multi-talented; you should be able to wear it in a variety of weather, and on a variety of occasions. Opt for layering pieces, rather than bulky ones: a cardigan and shell, for example, can be worn far more often than a heavy sweater. Choose simple silhouettes over fussy ones: a v-neck shirt coordinates with more pieces than a ruffled one. Select items that go with everything, instead of next to nothing: basic black pumps are infinitely more versatile than lime green stilettos.

Favor apparel that can be dressed up as well as down. Skip the sequins and sweatshirts, and any other items that'll be too dressy or too casual most of the time. Instead, choose the sweater that goes from the office to dinner; the dress that can be glamorized with a strand of pearls or relaxed with a pair of sandals; the shirt that works with a suit and tie and also with jeans. Want to add some pizzazz? Do like the ever-fashionable French, and use chic accents–like a sharp tie, statement belt, or bold bracelet–to liven up simple, classic clothes. I've noticed that if I add an eye-catching scarf to an old ensemble, someone will invariably comment on my "new outfit." Such is the power of accessories–they freshen up a tired look in no time flat and require very little storage space.

CONTAIN

Keep all your clothes in a closet, dresser, armoire, or shelving unit. Don't let your shoes lounge in the living room or your shirts hide in your spouse's closet. To that end, give everything a place: dedicate certain shelves to t-shirts, certain drawers to underwear, and certain sections of the closet to coats, suits, and dresses. In your Inner Circle, store the items you wear on a daily or weekly basis–like your socks, underwear, pajamas, work clothes, weekend clothes, exercise clothes, and around-the-house clothes. Keeping them accessible saves you time getting dressed and makes them easy to put away.

Reserve your Outer Circle for clothes you wear less frequently–from once or twice a month to once or twice a year. Dress clothes and formal attire will likely reside here. Why keep them if you seldom wear them? Because chances are you'll be invited to a wedding, holiday party, or other social function, and it's less stressful to have something on hand than to go shopping. That doesn't mean you need three tuxedos or five ball gowns; one suit or little black dress may suffice. Because such occasions are rare, you can usually get away with repeating an outfit. Your Outer Circle may also contain specialty and seasonal clothes like ski pants and bathing suits. Move them into your Inner Circle at the appropriate time of year.

Very little (if any) clothing should be in Deep Storage. Sentimental items like wedding dresses are potential candidates, should you choose to keep them. You might also use Deep Storage to save children's clothes for a younger sibling. Just be careful where you store them: attic, basement, and garage spaces can be harsh on fabric, and speed them into your Trash pile. If possible, find a remote but climate-controlled spot inside the house.

If you consolidate your clothing into Modules, the results can be startling! You may discover that you have ten pairs of black pants, twenty white shirts, or thirty pairs of shoes. When you see them all together, you'll quickly realize you have *more* than enough. The idea is to *keep* them consolidated, so you're never tempted to add to your collection. Hang all your skirts together, pants together, dresses together, and coats together. Keep pajamas, workout clothes, and sweaters stacked on their own shelves, and socks and underwear stashed in their own drawers.

If you'd like, you can further break down your "category" Modules by color, season, or type. For example, store all your navy pants, brown blazers, or khaki shorts together. You can break down your shirts into sleeveless, short sleeve, and long sleeve, and your skirts into mini, knee-length, and ankle-length. You can divide your dresses into casual and formal, and your suits into summer and winter weight. The more specific your Modules, the easier it is to take stock of what you own. Do the same for accessories; just because they're small, they shouldn't be forgotten. Consolidate your scarves, and divide them into seasons. Consolidate your shoes, and divide them by activity (how many pairs of sneakers do you have?). Consolidate your jewelry, and divide it into earrings, necklaces, brooches, rings, and bracelets. Consolidate your handbags, and divide them by color, season, or function.

Once you've gathered everything together, it's time to cull. If you discover you have too many items in a single category, keep only the finest and most flattering–that's probably what you'll end up wearing anyway. Having some multiples is understandable; few people can get by with a single shirt or pair of pants. Even Buddhist monks typically have two robes! The problem occurs when you have so many similar items that you barely wear most of them. Choose your best and most beautiful, and declutter the rest.

Finally, contain your clothes so they stay in order. That doesn't mean you have to run out and buy twenty plastic bins–you can simply keep them on a certain shelf, in a certain drawer, or in a certain section of your closet. Small items, however, are best stored in actual containers: use trays, boxes, or baskets for things like pantyhose, scarves, watches, and jewelry. It'll keep them organized and keep a lid on their accumulation.

In this era of mass production, clothing is inexpensive and readily available; we can go on a shopping spree and come back with a carload, if we're so inclined. Furthermore, fashion is always changing; what's "in" this season is "out" the next, only to be replaced by a new set of must-have items. While our great-grandparents could only obtain a few new pieces each year, we have no such restrictions. No wonder our closets are bursting at the seams!

When we update our wardrobes, we must also purge them of the outdated, the outgrown, and the out-of-favor.

That's why Limits play such an important role in our minimalist wardrobes; they keep our apparel and accessories to a manageable level. In the largest sense, then, limit your clothing to the available storage space—don't let it pour out of your closet and into the room. Better yet: instead of stuffing your closet to the breaking point, remove enough items to create some breathing room. It's not good for your clothes (or stress levels) when you have to wrestle them from hangers or squash them into drawers. With that in mind, let's revise the above statement: limit your clothing to *less* than the available storage space.

I certainly can't tell you how many shirts, sweaters, or pairs of pants you should own—that number is for you to decide. When I moved overseas, I could only fit four pairs of shoes in my luggage; hence, that's what I kept. When I bought a hanger that held five skirts, I capped my collection at that number. I've limited my coats to one per season, and my socks and underwear to a ten-day supply. Your Limits will be different from mine and depend on your personal situation and comfort level. Have fun seeing how many outfits you can make from a fixed number of items–it's a great opportunity to exercise your creativity and style.

Fashion changes faster than our clothes wear out; so if we purchase new items each season, our closets fill up quickly. Therefore, when we update our wardrobes, we must also purge them of the outdated, the outgrown, and the out-of-favor. Apply the One-In-One-Out rule and make a like-for-like trade: if you bring home a new pair of sneakers, make an old pair take a hike; if you splurge on a new dress, waltz an old one out the door; if you buy a new business suit, send an old one into retirement. Your wardrobe will then be a fresh, ever-changing collection, rather than a stale archive of fashions past.

And if your old clothes are "too good" to get rid of, question if you really need anything new. What's the point of adding to your wardrobe if your current apparel is perfectly adequate? Don't feel pressured to keep up with fashion trends–they're nothing more than a marketing ploy, designed to separate you from your hard-earned money. Instead of buying each season's must-haves, invest in classic pieces that stay in style. You'll have a bigger bank account, a more spacious closet, and a lot less decluttering to do.

MAINTAIN

We've freed up space in our closets, and learned to look gorgeous with less. Let's congratulate ourselves on a job well done! Now we have to make sure that things don't get out of hand again.

First of all, keep your closet tidy. As soon as you take off an article of clothing, hang it, fold it, or toss it in the hamper. By storing things in their appropriate Modules, you'll always have a good grasp of what you own–and eliminate the chance that five new sweaters will sneak their way in. Keep the floor of your closet empty by using vertical storage, like shelves, shoe racks, closet rods, or hanging organizers. It keeps the clutter from creeping in and your clothes in better condition. When you're getting dressed for a job interview or first date, the last thing you want to do is pluck your blouse or blazer off the closet floor.

Second, take care of your clothes; you can't afford to have a crucial item sidelined by a mud splatter or frayed hem. Use common sense to avoid damage: don't wear your suede shoes in the rain or your white pants to your kid's soccer game. A bit of preventative maintenance goes a long way: fix small tears before they become big ones, and treat stains before they turn stubborn. When you give your clothes a little TLC, you won't need backups waiting in the wings.

Third, stay out of the stores. Don't shop for fun, for entertainment, or out of sheer boredom–that's when you get into trouble! You know how it goes: you're wandering through a department store, and a cute dress catches your eye. Forty-five minutes later, you're walking out the door with it–plus matching shoes, handbag, wrap, earrings, and a few more pieces you picked up along the way. Avoid temptation, and don't set foot in a store (or surf a retailer's website) until you absolutely *need* something. Make an inventory of your clothing, and take it with you when you go shopping; if you have twenty-three shirts on your list, you'll be much less likely to buy a twenty-fourth.

Finally, declutter with the change of seasons. Autumn and spring are wonderful times to re-evaluate your wardrobe. When you're hauling out your coats or sweaters in preparation for winter, take some time to go through them. Our tastes change, our bodies change, and so does fashion. That jacket you loved last year might look worn, outdated, or unappealing to you now, or those skinny jeans may have become a bit *too* skinny since you last wore them. Purge anything you don't think you'll wear, and start the new season with some extra closet space!

24
Home office

Now we'll get down to some serious work: decluttering our offices. We'll dig out our desks from the mountains of paperwork, and devise systems to prevent future pileups. It may sound daunting, but we'll take it one step at a time–and I promise, it's a lot more fun than paying bills or doing taxes. Furthermore, the rewards will be well worth the effort: your new, clean, magnificent space will make you a million times more productive!

Imagine that you're sitting at your desk, hard at work on an important project. You're making good progress, when you suddenly find need for a specific document. "Uh-oh," you think, eyeing the piles of papers scattered on your desk. You clench your teeth and dive in, praying it'll materialize without too much effort. No such luck. You page through the stacks with increasing desperation–in the meantime uncovering a bill that needs to be paid, a form that needs to be mailed, and a receipt that needs to be filed. You take care of these matters, then resume your search; when you're about to call the document "lost," you spot it in another pile across the room. But by that time, your concentration is broken and your time is short; the project will have to wait, unfinished, for another day.

When your space is clear, your mind is clear–you can work without distraction and be more productive. A sloppy desk, on the other hand, is a roadblock to progress. If your space is too chaotic, you may not get any work done at all!

So how do we Start Over? Here, more than anywhere, it helps to break the task into smaller pieces. Rather than move our desks, bookcases, and filing cabinets into the hall, we'll attack the *contents* of these items first. If we can reduce them so much as to eliminate a piece of furniture, fantastic! However, papers and office supplies are small and numerous; one drawer, or one file folder, may be all you're able to tackle at once. Don't be tempted to rush through it; take the time to be thorough, and your efforts will have much greater impact.

Totally empty out your drawer or shelf of choice. Instead of picking out an item or two to purge, channel your inner dump truck and completely upset its contents. Once everything's laid out, you can give each item due consideration and decide whether it's truly worth keeping. If you've ever fantasized about playing an all-powerful deity, here's your chance:

the fate of hundreds of staples, paperclips, pens, papers, and rubber bands lies in your hands. Work your divine magic, and create a minimalist paradise!

In the process, think carefully about how and where you store your paperwork and supplies. Just because your stapler has always been in the far left corner of your second drawer doesn't mean it has to return there. Starting Over is a wonderful opportunity to mix things up and try a new configuration–a chance to design your workspace for maximum ease and efficiency.

DECLUTTER

First, start with the easy stuff: get rid of all the junk mail that's accumulated. The vast majority of this stuff–credit card applications, sales circulars, catalogs, brochures, and flyers–has little significance in the grand scheme of things. If it's not important enough to act on *now*, show it the recycling bin. Don't labor over decision-making, just go on and purge like nobody's business. It's highly unlikely you'll live to regret tossing a piece of junk mail.

While you're at it, throw out (or recycle) everything that's clearly Trash: dried-up pens, rusty paperclips, stretched-out rubber bands, spent erasers, outdated calendars, broken pencils, torn file folders, old sticky notes, used envelopes, empty ink cartridges, and anything unidentifiable. I don't know how damaged and decrepit office supplies slip below our radar and hang around so long. Gather them up, and put them out of their misery.

That was a good warm-up, wasn't it? Didn't it feel great to clear out all that stuff? Now that we're psyched up and in the groove, we're ready for bigger challenges. You may not realize it, but some of your "good" office supplies should also be in the Trash pile. Before you cry "Heresy!" let me explain. Office supplies build up over time–often, over a *long* time–and we seldom clear them out. During that period, technology, tastes, and needs change, leaving some of those items decidedly less useful.

To have a truly minimalist office, Narrow Down your supplies to the bare essentials.

I'm embarrassed to admit it, but during my last major purge, I uncovered a package of photo corners (my pictures are all digitized), a box of floppy disks, VHS labels, and–believe it or not–typewriter correction tape. I'm sure I'm not the only one who's discovered outmoded supplies in a modern workspace; dig deep, and you may unearth a few antiquities of your own. These items may still be functional, but they're largely obsolete, and if they're of no use to you, or anyone else, you know where they belong.

While we're talking Trash, here's something else to add: broken computer and electronic equipment. In most cases, we've already replaced these items with bright, shiny new ones. So why does our lifeless monitor still reside in the far corner of the office? Do we really expect to revive it if our new one suddenly fails? Most of us don't have the technological prowess to fix such items, and the repair cost often exceeds the replacement cost. So if you're still housing a printer, computer, or other equipment that has long since given up the ghost, say your final farewell. Don't make your office a retirement home for old and outdated machines.

Further candidates for your Trash pile are paperwork and supplies related to past projects and interests. If you're no longer involved with them, set the stuff free. I know that it's tempting to retain such items as proof of your hard work. That's exactly how I felt about my graduate school notebooks; they represented the blood, sweat, and tears of an arduous course of study. However, the information contained therein was irrelevant to my new career. The day the recycling truck hauled them away, I felt a hundred pounds lighter–and ready to embrace my future instead of hold on to my past.

As you're evaluating your stuff, make generous use of your Transfer pile. Even though *you* no longer need fifty fluorescent file folders or a lifetime supply of No. 2 pencils, someone else might, and that someone may be a school, hospital, or nonprofit, whose money is better spent providing services than buying office supplies. Computer and electronic equipment can be particularly valuable to such organizations. Make some phone calls and offer up your excess–the time and effort to find it a new home is worth the good karma. Save your donation receipts, and take a tax write-off if possible.

Now that you've purged the battered, the broken, and the obsolete, take a careful look at the leftovers. Ask hard questions to determine your Treasures. Do you really need five different colors of highlighters or six different kinds of envelopes? How many ways do you need to tell the date and time (if you have a watch, computer, and cell phone, are a desk clock and calendar necessary)? Does the paperweight do its job, or just hang around looking pretty? These may seem like trivial items, but they can add up to significant desk space.

To have a truly minimalist office, Narrow Down your supplies to the bare essentials. If you mail only ten envelopes a year, you don't need five hundred on hand. If you rarely require a rubber band, eliminate the stash in your desk drawer. How many staplers, rulers, tape dispensers, pencil sharpeners, and pairs of scissors do you have? If the answer is more than one, it's too many! Things like staplers don't need understudies; in the rare case they fail, they can be replaced cheaply and easily. Don't devote valuable space to storing backups.

In this day and age, there's little need to stock up. Almost anything you require can be readily obtained at your local store or on the Internet–it's like having a giant, on-demand, off-site supply closet. Find your own comfort level: if you feel you can't work without a five-year supply of paper or printer cartridges, so be it. But if your space is tight or your storage sparse, know that you probably *can* get by with less. At the very least, it's a fun experiment–and the earth won't stop spinning if you run short on paperclips.

With a little creativity, you can also Narrow Down your office equipment. Make your laptop your primary computer, and ditch the separate desktop. Choose multi-functional devices–such as a printer that also scans and photocopies–instead of finding space for three separate machines. Challenge yourself to get the job done with the least amount of equipment.

Finally, call up all your minimalist might and turn it loose on your paperwork. For this purpose, I highly recommend a scanner–it'll take up less space than the stacks of paper it eliminates. You'll wonder how you ever lived without this wondrous device! I digitize articles, greeting cards, letters, bills, statements, instructions, photos, pamphlets, and more–anything for which I need the information, but not the original copy. (Of course, be diligent about purging computer files, so you don't end up with digital clutter.) But before you go too crazy with the scanner, understand that you'll always need to keep *some* paper copies. Specific time frames for retaining documents are dependent on your personal situation, tax and legal requirements, and common practice in your area. Consult your financial advisor or the Internet for up-to-date details.

In the future, think long and hard before you print *anything*–why generate more paper to deal with down the road? Leave emails in your inbox, and bookmark web pages for future reference. If you're worried you won't be able to access the information later, print it to a PDF file. That way, you'll have a copy on your hard drive and can view it anytime. This strategy is ideal for online receipts and payment confirmations–it provides the proof you need without all the clutter. Just be sure to back up your files regularly to prevent any data loss.

CONTAIN

A place for everything, and Everything In Its Place is the single best way to keep a tidy desk. Instead of letting pens, paperclips, and rubber bands run wild in your workspace, corral them into designated spots and *make sure they stay there*. Assign specific places for file folders, incoming mail, outgoing mail, catalogs, magazines, receipts, and every category of office supply and paperwork you have. If it helps, label containers, drawers, and shelves to remind you of their appropriate contents.

A place for everything, and Everything In Its Place is the single best way to keep a tidy desk.

Your Inner Circle should consist of regularly used supplies and active paperwork. That means pens, pencils, paperclips, envelopes, stamps, notepads, checkbook, and incoming and outgoing mail (among other things) should be within arm's reach. In your Outer Circle belongs paperwork and files with which you've recently dealt and may need to reference again (like bills, receipts, statements, and research materials), and backup supplies like printer paper and ink cartridges. Use Deep Storage for paperwork that must be retained long-term or indefinitely–like birth and marriage certificates, diplomas, deeds, tax returns, and other essential legal and financial documents. Don't be tempted to digitize and declutter them, as you'll usually need the originals. Stow them out of the way, and consider a fireproof box or safety deposit box for those that are hard to replace.

As you make your Modules, give each category of office supply its own special container (even if it's just a ziplock bag or slot in a drawer organizer). Paperclips shouldn't be partying with the rubber bands, stamps shouldn't be socializing with the staples, and files shouldn't be fraternizing with magazines and catalogs. Consolidation helps you find them faster and illuminates the excess. When you've gathered thirty pencils into one place, you'll realize the absurdity of having so many–and hopefully be inspired to let most of them go.

Alternatively, organize your supplies by activity–it can boost productivity by ensuring you have the necessary supplies on hand for regular tasks. Examples include a bill-paying Module, in which you keep your checkbook, envelopes, stamps, and pen; a tax return Module, in which you gather all relevant receipts and documentation throughout the year; or project Modules, in which you store materials and paperwork needed for specific business, research, or writing endeavors.

As you consolidate, you'll likely find you have more pens, paperclips, staples, rubber bands, and other miscellaneous items than you'll ever realistically use. It's not necessarily your fault; many of these items are sold only in bulk quantities. Others, like pens, follow you home from the office, jump into your bag while you're out and about, and multiply under cover of night. Set Limits for each category, declutter the excess, and in the future keep a minimalist mindset when shopping for supplies. Pass on the super-size packages or split such purchases with a friend, family member, or colleague.

Modules and Limits also keep paperwork under control. We know what happens when we file, and file, and file some more: we end up with bulging folders, whose contents spill into more folders, and before we know it, we're buying another filing cabinet. Filing should be a two-way street: stuff should come *out*, as well as go in. To this end, limit your paperwork by topic to what will fit in one folder–and when it gets too fat, purge its contents. Use the One-In-One-Out rule to make it even easier: when you file a new bill or statement, throw the oldest on record away (assuming you don't need it for tax, financial, or legal purposes).

If you lack a dedicated workspace, your whole office may be a Module. We're not all blessed with an extra bedroom or dining room to use as a home office. Some may be relegated to a desk in the corner of the living room, or a retrofitted closet; others may carry their entire "office" in a tote bag or plastic bin, using any available surface as flex space. How wonderful would it be, actually, to reduce our office supplies, files, and equipment to a portable container? Then, when the sun is shining and birds are chirping, we can set up shop on our front porch, backyard, or local park. Ah, the minimalist dream!

MAINTAIN

In your office, it's supremely important to keep All Surfaces Clear. Treat your desk as flex space, and clean it off when you wrap up each day's work–as if someone else might come in and use it tomorrow. (Of course, it'll only be you, but wouldn't it be lovely to sit down at a clean space?) Keep office supplies in drawers or containers instead of scattered across the desk; invest in a standing or wall-mounted rack to hold incoming paper and mail, and use a bulletin board for reminders, cards, notes, and random scraps of paper, rather than let them invade your workspace.

An amazing (and distressing) thing happens in office spaces: everything that provides the least bit of horizontal space starts collecting stuff. I've seen stacks of papers and supplies perched on shelves, filing cabinets, window ledges, printers, scanners, chairs, lamps, boxes, and planters. Please, resist the urge to "paper" your surroundings; it's chaotic, it's unorganized, and it makes it almost impossible to find stuff. Clear surfaces are not only pleasing to the eye, they're beneficial to the mind. You'll be able to think more clearly and work more productively without all the visual distraction.

Furthermore, it shouldn't have to be said, but I'll say it all the same: the floor is not a filing system. But you know what happens: once those other surfaces are filled to the brim, the overflow lands on that big flat surface underfoot. Office floors are fertile ground; they'll sprout stacks of books, magazines, and paperwork that grow into forests. I usually recommend some tough-love decluttering over additional storage, but if you've truly run out of space, better to get another filing cabinet than wade through papers to get to your desk.

We can declutter all we want, but one of the keys to a minimalist office is controlling the *inflow*. In the rest of the house, this power lies entirely in our hands; we can effectively shut the door on stuff. The problem: in that door lies a mail slot. And through that slot will pour all kinds of useless, unwanted, and uninvited clutter, almost every single day. Let's focus our efforts on stopping this postal deluge.

> Clear surfaces are not only pleasing to the eye, they're beneficial to the mind.

You can eliminate the bulk of your junk mail by putting a freeze on your credit report or registering with OptOutPrescreen.com (a joint venture of the major credit reporting agencies). Once you do, companies will no longer be able to run credit checks on your name and send you pre-approved offers. You can also contact the Direct Marketing Association (www.the-dma.org) and request they add your name to their "Do Not Mail" database. Additionally, review the Privacy Policies that come with your bank and credit card statements; call the provided number, and tell them you *don't* want to receive marketing materials from them or their partner companies.

Henceforth, guard your name and address like a closely held secret. Don't sign up for in-store rewards programs and discount cards, and decline to provide your information at the checkout register. Don't participate in surveys, sweepstakes, and giveaways–more often than not, they're sneaky ways for marketers to snag your contact details. Don't send in product registration and warranty cards. When you move, don't fill out post office change of address forms, or your junk mail will surely follow you to your new home. Instead, personally contact people and companies to provide them with your new address. Rather than subscribe to newspapers and magazines, read them online. And by all means, don't request catalogs; if you sign up for one, you'll be getting them from thirty different companies by the end of the year.

The above strategies will eliminate most of your unsolicited mail. If you'd like, you can also limit incoming paperwork from companies you do business with, and opt to receive electronic communications instead. For example, sign up for online billing. You can even choose to have the amount you owe automatically debited from your bank account. Similarly, register to receive bank and credit card statements online. By doing so, you'll avoid the advertisements and offers that come stuffed in the envelopes and reduce the paperwork you have to file.

Our offices are dynamic spaces; there's stuff coming in, stuff going out, and stuff moving around on a daily basis. Therefore, we can't simply do a large-scale declutter and call it a day. Keeping this area streamlined requires constant vigilance.

To that end, be a good gatekeeper: keep a recycling bin by the front door, and stop catalogs, circulars, takeout menus, and other junk mail from even entering the house. For the mail that makes it into your office: open each piece and *act* on it immediately, instead of stacking it up on your desk. Shred credit card solicitations, balance transfer checks, and other nonessential paper with personal information; scan or file any documents you need to keep; sort bills that require payment, letters that require action, or information that requires review into the appropriate inbox or slot on your desk. In an ideal system, each piece of paper would be handled just once.

When you finish your work for the day, return all supplies to their designated places and files to their appropriate folders. If it's more efficient to keep them together, set up a "working" Module for that particular project–preferably in some kind of container, rather than spread out across your desk. Then, you can pick up right where you left off, without having to gather up the necessary materials; and you won't have to push them aside to use your desk in the meantime. Also, be on the lookout for refugee items from elsewhere in the house. Return your child's homework, your spouse's novel, or your dog's chew toy to its respective owner before it has a chance to settle in. You have enough to worry about with your own stuff.

Everyday Maintenance will keep your desk clear and your stuff under control. However, you'll still need to purge your files periodically. Try as you might to follow the One-In-One-Out rule, chances are you'll still end up with a little more "in" than "out." Scan your file folders on a monthly or quarterly basis, and toss (that is, shred or recycle) what's no longer relevant. Furthermore, do a full-scale purge on an annual basis, and clear out the old to make way for the new. I like to schedule this for early January and have a fresh start for the new year!

25
Kitchen and dining room

If asked to name the most functional room in the house, many of us would choose the kitchen. After all, it's the place where we store, prepare, serve, and often consume the food that sustains us. It also serves as a popular gathering place for the family. Given its significant role in our lives, no wonder the kitchen contains a lot of stuff! Too much stuff, however, can diminish the room's functionality, and make it unpleasant to work and hang out in. So let's see how we can pare things down, and make this space as streamlined as possible.

Have you ever wandered through a kitchen showroom (or browsed through the pages of your favorite decorator magazine) and fantasized about trading in your kitchen for the one on display? Did you eye its gleaming surfaces with envy, thinking how wonderful it would be to cook in such a sleek and functional environment?

Much of the time, what attracts us to showroom kitchens isn't the high-end appliances, specialty countertops, or fancy cabinetry–it's the space! Display kitchens are invariably clean, spare, and free of clutter, and have little more than a handful of appliances and tableware. That's what makes them so lovely and inviting. The good news: you don't have to spend a fortune on renovations to achieve this look. You can give your kitchen a dramatic makeover simply by decluttering.

To Start Over, empty every drawer, cabinet, cupboard, and shelf in turn. As always, don't be tempted to leave something in place because you "know" you will put it back there. Remove every piece, until the space in question is bare–that means all your plates, coffee cups, glassware, forks, spoons, knives, pots, pans, gadgets, appliances, food, foil, takeout containers, and even the contents of your "junk" drawer. Remember, the idea is not to choose the things we'll get rid of, but to choose the things we'll keep. Once everything's out, you're going to examine it thoroughly, and return only your best, most useful, and most essential items to their places. Pretend you're outfitting a brand-new dream kitchen, like the ones featured in magazines. Why should yours be any less fabulous?

Should you have any lingering doubts about clearing the contents, this method yields a special bonus: the fantastic opportunity to *clean* those cabinets. How long has it been since they've had a good scrubbing? In the course of cooking, kitchens get greasy and dirty, and while we're pretty good at keeping the surfaces sparkling, we tend to forget about the *insides* of our cabinets. So while you're eliminating the clutter, eliminate the dirt as well (how efficient we minimalists are!). Scrub them spotless, and you'll truly have a fresh start!

DECLUTTER

As you're cleaning out your kitchen, you'll probably come across plenty of items for your Trash pile. If you haven't purged your pantry lately, much of it may be food; check the expiration dates of every item you touch, and ditch anything that's spoiled, expired, or otherwise past its prime. Spices, sauces, and condiments also have limited shelf lives, so don't let your decluttering pass them by. If that bottle of soy sauce is older than your toddler, toss it and treat yourself to a new one when needed. Do the same for other perishables, particularly if you can't remember how long you've had them, or the last time you used them.

Other Trash may also be lurking in your kitchen–in the form of chipped plates, cracked glasses, and bent or mangled silverware (like the fork that got caught in the garbage disposal). Give your food the respect it deserves, and serve it on (and with) undamaged tableware. Don't save these battered pieces as backups for your better stuff. Discard broken gadgets and appliances, too; if you haven't yet made the effort to repair them, you evidently can live without them.

In your Transfer pile belong all those items that are useful to someone other than *you*. For some reason, we tend to accumulate much more kitchenware than we need or use on a daily basis. Some of it enters our lives as wedding and housewarming gifts, others as impulse purchases. Some items may have seemed practical when we purchased them, but turned out to be too complicated or time-consuming for our lifestyles; so give that pasta machine or ice cream maker to someone who'll appreciate it. Be honest with yourself as you're sorting through your stuff; if you avoid using your food processor because it's a pain to clean, take this opportunity to set it free.

Don't forget that food can go into your Transfer pile as well. Our tastes and dietary needs change over time, and the shelf life of some foods can outlast our desire for them. We may grow tired of tomato soup before we finish our stash, or decide we'd rather eat fresh fruit than the canned stuff on our shelves. Don't feel bad; regard it as a wonderful chance to do a good deed! Donate any unwanted canned or packaged items to a local food bank or soup kitchen. The castoffs from your pantry can keep someone else from going hungry.

You may have difficulty purging some kitchen items out of concern that you'll need them someday (and you're pretty sure it'll be the day after you get rid of them). If so, create a Temporarily Undecided box. Put in it those things you don't use regularly, but think you *might* use sometime soon—like the bread machine, muffin tins, and fancy cake decorating supplies. Mark the box with a date, and donate whatever you don't retrieve after a specific period of time (say six months, or a year). It's a good way to deal with those "on-the-fence" items; they're available if necessary, but won't take up precious space in your cabinets and drawers. Better yet, you'll see what life is like without them—and you may decide you don't miss them at all.

In your Transfer pile belong all those items that are useful to someone other than *you*.

The kitchen is a great place to have a conversation with your stuff. Some items have been lurking in the shadows for so long, you may not know them anymore. Here's your chance to get reacquainted, and make sure your relationship is still mutually beneficial.

What are you and what do you do? We shouldn't have to ask, but let's admit it—sometimes we don't have a clue. These days, there's a kitchen gadget for every conceivable task, and just because that pineapple corer or pastry wheel seemed indispensable when we bought it, doesn't mean we'll be able to identify it a few years later. In this case, a little mystery is not a good thing. If you don't know what something does, it's obviously not essential in your kitchen. Send it on to another home–it could make a fun gift for a culinary friend, who might actually know what to do with it.

How often do I use you? Ah, the million-dollar question! Items that answer "every day" or "once a week" can make their way back into your cabinets. But just because you use the turkey baster only once a year doesn't mean you have to get rid of it; the knowledge can help you decide where to store it. For items used less than annually, some deliberation is in order: are they really worth the space they're taking up?

Do you make my life easier (or more difficult)? Sure, I can cook rice and boil water on the stovetop, but my rice cooker and tea kettle make my life easier. Therefore, they earn a spot in my kitchen. On the other hand, I let go of my cappuccino machine because I hated cleaning it, and found it much more pleasant to go out for a cup. If something's difficult to set up, use, or clean up (and the rewards are not worth the effort), consider giving it the heave-ho.

Do you have a twin? Kitchen items are like office supplies, in that they seem to reproduce of their own accord. Unless you're extremely dexterous, you can't use more than one potato peeler or can opener at a time. Furthermore, should one fail, you can easily acquire another. Ditch the doubles, and free up the space for something more useful.

Are you too good to use? I bet your stuff didn't see this one coming! Wedding china and heirloom silverware can become pretty smug, assuming they can hang around for decades doing nothing. Oftentimes, they're right: they get tucked away in dining hutches, and rarely see the light of day. We're too sentimental to get rid of them, and too scared to use them (lest we break or lose a piece). Here's a radical thought: instead of the full service, keep only one or two place settings–use them as decoration, or for romantic candlelight dinners with your spouse.

I wish I could provide a master list of the contents of a minimalist kitchen. Unfortunately, such an endeavor would be futile–mainly because we all have different ideas of what is necessary. It would be unfair to say you can't be a minimalist if you have a bundt pan or a deep fryer. That said, I think most of us can get by with fewer kitchen "essentials" than are generally published in cookbooks and magazines.

My husband and I have found we can prepare all our meals with just four pieces of cookware: a large skillet, a saucepan, a pasta pot, and a baking pan. Our small appliances are limited to a microwave, tea kettle, rice cooker, and French press (in place of a coffee maker). In terms of other implements, we own a chef's knife, bread knife, paring knife, colander, steamer, cutting board, measuring cup, spatula, serving spoon, whisk, can opener, corkscrew, cheese grater, stainless steel mixing bowl, and a water filtration pitcher. Some of you may find our list inadequate, while others may find it excessive. For us, however, it's perfectly *enough*.

Choose multi-functional items over single-use ones.

It's up to you to determine your own "enough"–and Narrow Down your culinary apparatus accordingly. To do so, choose multi-functional items over single-use ones. Unless you use them often, things like cherry pitters, melon ballers, bagel slicers, pizzelle irons, lobster shears, strawberry hullers, and crepe makers don't usually justify the space they command in your kitchen cabinets. Instead, favor simple implements that can perform a variety of functions. Similarly, a full range of skillets and saucepans isn't compulsory; one or two in popular sizes is sufficient.

Likewise, refrain from accumulating tableware in specialty sizes and shapes (like egg cups and sushi plates), and opt for versatile, all-purpose dishes. Instead of storing both "good" china and "everyday" china, choose one set and use it for all occasions. Pare down glassware as well. If you're not running a restaurant, you don't need a different vessel for every liquid–like wine glasses, champagne glasses, whiskey glasses, beer glasses, martini glasses, water glasses, and juice glasses. I have one set of simple tumblers that suffice for all beverages (other than coffee and tea), and to be honest, I prefer them to spindly glasses and flutes for wine and champagne.

While streamlining your kitchen, keep in mind that in some cultures, an extraordinary variety of cooking is done with the simplest of implements. It's our creativity in the kitchen–not the cookware in our cabinets–that make for delicious, satisfying meals. Good food doesn't come from fancy plates and fussy serving ware; it comes from the hands and the heart, and–as any Buddhist monk will tell you–can be just as well enjoyed in one simple bowl.

CONTAIN

To keep things organized and efficient, determine where you perform certain tasks–like prepping, cooking, serving, dining, washing up, and waste disposal–and store related tools and equipment accordingly. For example, keep the knives where you chop, the pots near the stove, and the dishwashing liquid under the sink. Confine miscellaneous tasks like bill paying to a particular place, to prevent pens and checkbooks from piling up on the counter or finding their way into your spice drawer.

Reserve a specific spot for every last item. The plates should be stacked just so, and the cups and glasses should fall into place like a chorus line. Forks, knives, spoons, pots, pans, and appliances should all have assigned seats. If it helps, stick little labels ("pasta pot," "sauce pan," "cereal bowls") to remind you (and family members) exactly where everything goes.

Allot items to your Inner Circle, Outer Circle, and Deep Storage. Your Inner Circle should contain the plates, pots, pans, utensils, drinkware, gadgets, appliances, and food you use on a regular basis. Dedicate to them your most easily accessible storage spots; you shouldn't have to get on a stepladder to retrieve your coffee mug, or cross the room to get your paring knife. In your Outer Circle–higher cabinets, lower drawers, and deeper corners–store items you use less than once a week, but more than once a year. Potential candidates include cake pans, crock pots, salad spinners, waffle irons, and cookie sheets.

In Deep Storage belong the items that emerge once a year or less (typically around the holidays)–like turkey roasters, punch bowls, gravy boats, soufflé dishes, dessert stands, serving platters, and specialty linens. Store these in the highest, lowest, and farthest reaches of your kitchen or dining room. However, just because you can put things into Deep Storage doesn't mean you *have* to. If you don't really need them (or could borrow them if necessary), feel free to let them go.

Modules are particularly valuable in the kitchen, where duplicate supplies and excess ingredients are common. They reveal how certain items have accumulated (often unnoticed) over time. They make us ask questions like, "Why do we have eighteen drinking glasses for our family of four?" "Will we ever use twenty pairs of chopsticks?" and "Why do I need two meat thermometers, three corkscrews, or four jars of cinnamon?" Culling duplicates is quick and easy–we don't have to labor over decisions or worry about doing without something (we'll still have *one*, after all). It creates breathing room in our cabinets and drawers, making it infinitely easier to find what we need when we're cooking.

When making Modules, many of us find we have far more tableware than we actually need. Why? Because when we acquire a new set, we rarely toss the old. The pieces are usually still functional (we replace them for the sake of novelty, not necessity)–so they get stashed into the recesses of our cabinets "just in case" we need extras. Alternatively, we may inherit the newcomers or receive them as gifts, and feel obligated to provide them with a home. Consider limiting your plates, cups, bowls, glasses, and utensils to match the size of your family; if your household has only four people, why clutter your cabinets with sixteen place settings? Pare down to the latest, greatest, or most beautiful pieces, and remove the old to make way for the new.

Ah, but what about guests, you say! By all means, take your entertaining habits into consideration when culling your supplies. Figure out the maximum number of people you *regularly* entertain, and save enough tableware to accommodate the group. If you host bigger parties but once in a blue moon, you can rent or borrow what you need. Still not ready to relinquish your place settings? Limit those in your cabinets to your everyday needs, and put the rest in Deep Storage until required.

When you find a better cookbook for a certain cuisine, or better recipe for a certain dish, let go of the old one.

Limit appliances and gadgets to the ones you use often–and when you upgrade to new ones, give away the old. Don't clutter your cupboards with the toasters, blenders, and coffee makers of yore; a young couple or college student might be thrilled to take them. And rein in those ubiquitous plastic containers; they're potentially useful, but they pile up quickly. Pick a handful to keep and recycle the rest.

Unfortunately, no kitchen would be complete without the proverbial "junk" drawer–the place we put all those ketchup packets, takeout menus, batteries, birthday candles, twist ties, tea lights, sewing needles, scissors, plastic utensils, and other odd items that are too small, few, or uncategorizable to fit anywhere else. What can we do about this mishmash of stuff? Evaluate every last item, and gather those that make the cut into a "utility" Module (same drawer, new and improved name!). Contain related items in ziplock bags or slots of a drawer organizer. If everything is readily accessible, easily identifiable, and truly useful, there's no need to label it "junk."

Last, let's talk about recipes and cookbooks–many more seem to enter the house than leave it. They accumulate steadily over time, and rarely do we replace one–we simply add to our collection. Before we know it, we have more recipes than days in the year to cook! Rather than archive them all, keep your selection fresh. When you find a better cookbook for a certain cuisine, or better recipe for a certain dish, let go of the old one. Think of your collection as dynamic, rather than static; let it evolve to suit your tastes and diet as they change over time.

MAINTAIN

The kitchen is such a hub of activity, it requires not only Everyday Maintenance–but *all-day* maintenance!

Things can spiral out of control here *within hours* if we don't stay on top of them. Dirty plates, pots, and pans pile up in the sink; food, gadgets, and packaging pile up on the counter;

bills, homework, and newspapers pile up on the table; toys, backpacks, and grocery bags pile up on the floor; leftovers pile up in the refrigerator. Generally, the more members in your household, the more stuff that ends up in the kitchen. Eventually, the clutter can become so overwhelming you couldn't possibly prepare (or eat) a meal there. If there's no room to wash, chop, slice, dice, pare, and peel, you'll be more likely to throw some frozen fare in the microwave or stop for takeout.

Don't let clutter cheat you out of a healthy, home-cooked dinner–keep those kitchen surfaces clear! They should hold only those items you use daily (if that). Consider wall-mounted racks for spices, knives, and other implements, and hanging baskets for fruits and vegetables. Appliances that mount under upper cabinets–like microwaves, toaster ovens, and coffee makers–can also free up valuable space. For an attractive and functional kitchen, skip the cutesy tchotchkes and cookie jars, and opt for sleek and understated instead. I promise you this: simply getting all that clutter off the countertops will energize you and inspire you to work some culinary magic.

Furthermore, wipe the slate clean after every meal. When you're cooking, put away gadgets, equipment, and ingredients as soon as you're finished with them. After you've eaten, clear the table and counters of any remaining food or implements. Wash all the dishes or load them into the dishwasher immediately after use. Better to spend a few minutes cleaning up after each meal than face the task when preparing the next;

a stack of dirty dishes can quickly dampen your desire to cook. In fact, try to live by the following rule: never leave the kitchen with dishes in the sink. (At the very least, never go to bed with dishes in the sink.) It's wonderful to have a fresh start every day, but even better to have one every meal!

The kitchen is such a hub of activity, it requires not only Everyday Maintenance—but *all-day* maintenance!

The kitchen has long been considered the heart of the home, a place for families to gather and share quality time, but because it's such a happening hot spot, its counters are magnets for clutter. Make sure everyone who plops down a toy, book, newspaper, or piece of mail takes it with them when they leave the room. (Or warn them they may find it in your next casserole!) Be vigilant of the floor as well; when you're carrying heavy pots and hot liquids, things underfoot can be a recipe for disaster.

Finally, the kitchen is a fantastic place for a one-a-day declutter. In this room, *something* can always go, whether it's yesterday's newspaper or last week's leftovers. Make it a habit to scan your refrigerator, freezer, and pantry shelves regularly for expired or outdated items (or stuff you have no desire to eat), and dispose of them promptly. Commit to purging at least one item every day, whether it's spoiled food, an extra coffee mug, an orphaned utensil, a mismatched plate, or a seldom-used gadget. Your junk drawer alone could probably keep you going for a year. Just think–your cupboards will actually grow more spacious with each passing day!

26
Bathroom

Ready for something easy? Let's take the minimalist strategies we've learned and beautify our bathrooms. This room is typically the smallest in the house, with the least amount of storage–and compared to the living room, office, and kitchen, streamlining it is a breeze! With just a little effort and a few simple habits, you can create a space that soothes your soul while you brush your teeth.

In the other rooms we've decluttered, we've often had to break the job into smaller bits. In contrast, the diminutive size of our bathrooms makes for a much more manageable task–something we can likely undertake all at once. It has just a fraction of the floor, counter, and cabinet space of our other rooms, and serves significantly fewer functions. However, the lack of space means we have to be particularly mindful of how we organize and use the room. We're not out to determine how much stuff we can pack into it, but rather how *little* we really need in it. Our goal is to create a serene, spa-like ambience.

First, close your eyes and picture your ideal minimalist bathroom. Visualize the spare, clean countertop with nary a hairspray bottle or mascara tube in sight. Look around at the lovely, empty floor–no towels piled up in the corner or extra supplies crammed under the sink. Take a peek at the gleaming surfaces and carefully chosen cleansing products in the tub. Open the drawers and medicine cabinet, and admire the orderly lineup of toiletries and grooming supplies. Not a single thing looks out of place, nor are the items fighting for space. Let your gaze rest on the votive candle or single orchid adorning the countertop. Ah . . . you could spend all day in this calm, relaxing space.

Okay, back to reality. Better yet–let's make it a reality! Start Over, just as in your other rooms, by emptying out the contents of the drawers, shelves, and cabinets. Clear everything off the countertops. Don't forget about the tub or shower stall–take the soap, shampoo, shaving cream, razors, and caddies out of there, too. Carry it all from the bathroom and lay it out elsewhere (like on your bedroom floor, or dining room table) for examination. Decluttering is far more effective when you remove items from their usual spots and evaluate them out of context. As you determine exactly which things you need, you'll put them back, one by one.

DECLUTTER

When sorting your things into Trash, Treasure, and Transfer piles, go through the motions of your daily routine. Pretend that you're brushing your teeth, and put your toothbrush, toothpaste, and floss in the Treasure pile. Pretend you're washing your face, and add your cleanser and washcloth. Simulate shaving, putting on makeup, fixing your hair, and any other grooming activities you perform, and send the requisite supplies to join your other Treasures. This exercise reveals *exactly* which products you use every day, and therefore, what belongs in your bathroom. It also reveals which items you *don't* use, and prompts you to question why you're keeping them.

Some items belong in your Trash pile simply because of their age. Cosmetics you don't wear regularly, for example, may be past their prime before they're used up. While makeup is rarely marked with an expiration date, it does have a limited shelf life. Liquids and creams–especially those worn on or around the eyes–have a lifespan of three to six months, while powdered foundation, concealer, blush, and lipstick generally last for a year. The reason for their degradation: moisture breeds bacteria. Let them hang around too long, and skin irritation and infections can result when you use them.

Be similarly diligent about tossing old medication. Most drugs–both prescription and over-the-counter–have expiration dates on their labels or packaging. Consult your doctor or pharmacist with questions about specific medicines. When it's time to discard them, do so responsibly. Don't throw left-over medications in the trash (where they can be consumed by children or animals), or flush them down the toilet (where they can contaminate the water supply). Instead, return them to the pharmacy for proper disposal.

The best reason to keep something in your bathroom is that *you use it.*

The best reason to keep something in your bathroom is that *you use it.* Conversely, the best reason to declutter something from your bathroom is that *you don't use it.* As you sort through your items, set aside anything you haven't touched in the last six months. Unless you have a very good (i.e., medical) reason for keeping it, toss it and free up the cabinet space. If it's a perishable item, it may be reaching the end of its lifespan anyway.

An exception to this rule is emergency supplies. In this category, those "might need its" and "just in cases" are more than welcome. Keep a well-stocked first aid kit that includes bandages, gauze pads, adhesive tape, antibiotic cream, rubbing alcohol, thermometer, fever reducers, pain relievers, antihistamines, antidiarrheals, antacids, and more. It doesn't matter if you haven't used such things in six months or six years—keep them on hand, because you never know when you'll need them. (Of course, periodically check expiration dates and replace outdated medicines.)

The next best reason to retain an item is that *it works for you*. You know what I'm talking about: the shampoo that tames your frizzies, the cream that erases your wrinkles, or the eyeshadow that makes your baby blues pop. On the other hand, the next best reason to declutter an item is that *it doesn't work for you*—like that expensive moisturizer that irritated your skin. Just because you paid good money for it, doesn't mean you have to keep it—or force yourself to use it.

Finally, let's consider another not-so-good reason for admittance to your bathroom: *because it was free*. In this category fall those samples you get in the mail, the freebies you pick up at the cosmetics counter, and those miniature bottles of soap and shampoo you bring home from every hotel. I know these tiny toiletries are super-cute, but if you don't use them, they're nothing but super-cute clutter. Don't bring them home to your bathroom unless you truly intend to use them.

To create a minimalist bathroom, it helps to pare down our beauty and grooming routines. Specialty products can make our *toilette* complicated and time-consuming; suddenly we find ourselves involved in a five-step cleansing program, using three different anti-aging creams, or applying mud masks multiple times a week. We're curling our hair, straightening it, moussing it, gelling it, teasing it, scrunching it, or spraying it into place. We're concealing our flaws, highlighting our cheekbones, and lengthening our lashes. Whew! Getting ready in the morning can be a job unto itself!

Take a close look at your routine, and consider where you can cut back. I'm confident you'll look just as gorgeous doing *half* what you do now. If you scaled down your skin care to a splash of soap and water, you could ditch the fancy cleansers and toners. If you decided to age gracefully, you could jettison the wrinkle creams. If you kept your makeup minimal and haircut simple, you could toss a drawerful of products. Beauty doesn't come from a bottle–it comes from within. Instead of stockpiling miracle goop, opt for natural beauty boosters like exercise, a healthy diet, plenty of water, and a good night's sleep.

To Narrow Down further, choose multi-use products. Double duty favorites include shampoo and conditioner combos, tinted lip balms, hair and body washes, and moisturizers with sunscreen. Some common household items are also beauty workhorses. Baking soda, for example, can be used for exfoliating, tooth brushing, hand cleansing, foot soaking, and hair care. Olive oil can be used as a facial moisturizer, makeup remover, hair conditioner, cuticle treatment, and lip balm. Petroleum jelly softens hands, feet, elbows, and knees. Versatile products can help eliminate a cabinet full of lotions and potions.

Now let's talk towels. These things can multiply like nobody's business! Why? Because when we buy new ones, we rarely ever throw the old ones away. They're just so practical, we can't bring ourselves to do it. Our fresh ones get the place of honor on the towel rack, the former get stowed away as backups, and our linen closets grow more stuffed with each passing year. Scan your bathroom, linen closet, or wherever you store them, and take an inventory. How many do you have? How many people are in your household? If there's a big difference between those two numbers, you have some decluttering to do.

Decide just how many towels each member of the household needs. If you're an extreme minimalist, your magic number may be one; however, I think most people will feel more comfortable with two. With a second towel, you have a backup while doing laundry, and an extra for guests to use. Furthermore, limit your towels to one versatile size; bath towels can serve most needs, allowing you to dispense with the hand towels, face towels, and fingertip towels. The fewer you have to store, wash, and keep track of, the better.

Finally, because the bathroom is such a small, functional space, avoid any temptation to fill it with knickknacks. Save for a candle or small bowl of flowers, keep decorative items to a minimum. They'll get wet, they'll get dirty, and they'll get in the way of your beauty routine. You shouldn't have to worry about breaking something when you're blow-drying your hair. And as for reading material, bring it in with you and take it when you leave–the bathroom is not a library!

CONTAIN

Space in the bathroom can be tight, and storage can be scarce. Therefore, every item should have an assigned spot and stay in it–like troops lined up for battle, rather than the aftermath of a house party.

Allocate your stuff to your Inner Circle, Outer Circle, and Deep Storage. Your Inner Circle should hold the majority of things in your bathroom: in short, the stuff you use every day. Typical items might be your toothbrush, toothpaste, floss, facial wash, moisturizer, sunscreen, makeup, brush, comb, razor, shaving cream, cotton swabs, cotton balls, washcloth, and any towels you're currently using. Naturally, they should be within easy reach, to make for an efficient grooming routine. Your Outer Circle should contain the items you don't use quite as often: like curling irons, nose hair trimmers, first aid kits, hair clippers, and extra towels and toiletries. Use Deep Storage if you buy a particular item in bulk–like bath soap or toilet paper–and lack storage space in your bathroom.

As you're sorting through your sundries, consolidate like items into Modules. In each grouping, take a long, hard look at what you have. Chances are, you'll discover quite a few duplicates in the process; weed out those extra combs, tweezers, and nail clippers. You might discover you've accumulated eighteen colors of nail polish, or six different scented lotions. When you see them all together, it may seem a bit excessive! Question how many you really need, and pare down to your favorites.

> To create a truly minimalist medicine cabinet, try to restrict your toiletries to one of each product.

Once you've culled your bathroom supplies, use containers to corral loose items. Keep cosmetics in a makeup case, and hair accessories like clips, barrettes, and bobby pins in their own bag. Do the same with medicines, beauty creams, nail items, and other grooming implements. When they're rolling around in a drawer, it's hard to keep them from multiplying; plus, the disarray provides a great hiding place for other clutter. When they're stowed in separate containers, it's easier to find them, and keep them under control. You can even get fancy, and make your Modules do decorative duty as well: cotton balls, cotton swabs, and bath salts look gorgeous in glass apothecary jars and give your bathroom a chic, spa-like feel.

Assign a drawer or shelf to each family member who shares the bathroom; that way, everyone has a personal Module. It'll prevent your family's toiletries from becoming a jumbled mess. This strategy gives each person a defined space for their stuff, and nothing more. If your teenager's hair products or spouse's shampoos overflow their designated shelves, they'll have to store the excess elsewhere. If storage space is scarce, install hooks for family members to hang personal toiletry bags. This cuts down on counter clutter, and makes everyone responsible for their own stuff.

When you apply Limits in the bathroom, the magic number is *one*. To create a truly minimalist medicine cabinet, try to restrict your toiletries to one of each product: one shampoo, one conditioner, one cleanser, one toner, one moisturizer, one perfume, one aftershave, one body lotion, one toothpaste, one lipstick, one eyeshadow, one mascara, one blush, one nail polish, and so on. One of each means less clutter in your cabinets, and less to think about in the morning. One of each means less impact on the environment, in terms of both manufacturing and disposal. One of each means embracing the concept of *enough*.

To this end, use something up before you buy a new one. I know that's easier said than done; when we hear about that "perfect" night cream or "must-have" mascara, we can't get to the beauty aisle fast enough! Try to resist these impulse purchases, particularly if you have a similar product at home–or at least dispose of your old, half-finished, not-so-miraculous toiletry when you bring home a replacement. Don't feel obligated to hold on to its remnants, thinking you might go back and finish it someday; it'll probably go bad before you get to use it. Similarly, once you've started new ones, don't let those almost-empty toothpaste tubes and conditioner bottles hang around; it's unlikely you'll develop the superhuman strength needed to squeeze out the last remaining molecules. Keep tabs on your cosmetics as well. If you bring home a new lipstick from the fall palette, or a new eyeshadow from the spring collection, say "adiós" to last season's shades. A fresh selection is more fun than a cache of stale supplies.

MAINTAIN

Maintaining a streamlined bathroom is a piece of cake! In fact, it's a great place to hone your minimalist powers and gain the skills and confidence to take on the rest of the house.

You'll make your job a lot easier if you're a good gatekeeper. Constantly be on guard for wayward items–especially if you share the bathroom with other household members. Each time you exit the room, take with you anything that doesn't belong there: like your toddler's sippy cup, your teenager's sneakers, your spouse's copy of *Popular Mechanics*, or the book you were reading in the tub. Make sure no one is using the floor as an impromptu laundry basket or temporary storage spot; if so, orchestrate a prompt pickup or return of the stray possessions.

Clear surfaces are not only more attractive, they're more hygienic.

Ideally, keep your bathroom surfaces clear of all items when not in use. I know it's tempting to keep your toothbrush or deodorant out on the counter–you use them every day, after all–but clutter likes to socialize. Leave them out and before long, a hairbrush will sidle up to them; a razor will start hanging around; then, a lipstick, lotion, and bottle of perfume might join the fun. Multiply this by several family members, and your counters will get very crowded, very fast. In the end, it's easier to keep everything tucked away.

For the same reasons, absolutely nothing should be on your bathroom floor–no towels, laundry, or extra supplies. Gather dirty clothes in a hamper, and keep your surplus provisions in cabinets, baskets, or stackable bins (or in another part of the house). Use hooks and rods to hang up towels and bathrobes. Tub ledges should be clear as well; install a shelf or shower caddy instead of lining up your soap, shampoo, and shaving cream around the perimeter.

Clear surfaces are not only more attractive, they're more hygienic. Bathrooms are warm, moist, enclosed environments. Dirt, mildew, and germs thrive in such conditions, and will attach themselves to any available object; the fewer hosts we provide for them, the better. Countertops are much easier to clean when you don't have to worry about moving, or knocking over, an assortment of toiletries in the process.

At the very least, clear your surfaces before turning in for the night. Put all toiletries, tools, and tidbits back in their designated spots, hang up all towels, and give countertops a quick wipe-down. Make this a regular routine before falling into bed, and you'll awake to a beautiful minimalist bathroom each morning!

27
Storage spaces

Now that we've streamlined our living space, let's take a look at our storage spaces–like the attic, basement, and garage (or storage locker in your apartment or condo building). Oftentimes, this is where the clutter from the rest of the house ends up when we don't know what to do with it. However, just because it's out of sight doesn't mean it's out of mind.

Storage space seems like the answer to our problems; how orderly our lives would be if we had a full basement, big attic, or two-car garage to stash all our stuff! Unfortunately, however, this "solution" often backfires: stuff expands to fill the available space, and before we know it, we have more stuff than ever to deal with.

My husband and I once lived quite comfortably in a studio apartment, with no storage space other than a utility closet. Then we moved into a three-bedroom house with an attic, basement, and garage. Guess what happened? Our possessions increased exponentially! During our apartment years, whenever we tired of a piece of furniture, or sports and hobby equipment, we had to get rid of it–we simply had no place to store it. Once we moved into our house, these things wound up in the basement, "just in case" we needed them someday. Well, these "just in cases" piled up and piled up, creating an entirely new clutter problem. Frankly, I think it's easier to live minimally when you *don't* have any storage space!

To avoid clutter buildup, keep your storage space as streamlined as your living space. Just because you have a big garage doesn't mean you have to fill every square inch of it. Better to store your car in there than a bunch of things you don't use. What's more, these areas can serve as additional flex space: they're ideal places to pursue messy hobbies, and can even be converted into family rooms or bedrooms. Don't let useless junk prevent you from using them to their potential.

With storage spaces, you can Start Over in one of two ways: a little at a time, or the whole enchilada. If you're feeling ambitious, do it BIG! Devote an entire weekend to decluttering, and empty the contents of the basement, attic, or garage into your yard or driveway. It's easy to overlook things when they're lurking in dark corners; bring them out into the light for examination. Sometimes, simply moving an item out of the house helps you overcome the urge to keep it; suddenly it seems ridiculous to hang on to your old baseball cleats, or the broken bicycle you haven't ridden in years.

To avoid clutter buildup, keep your storage space as streamlined as your living space.

For best results, get the whole family involved and make a party of it. Play music, serve refreshments, and create a fun atmosphere, so it feels more like a game than a chore. For added incentive, make plans for how you'll use the "new" space; your teenager will embrace the project with much more enthusiasm if it results in a home theater or place for his band to practice.

Alternatively, if a major purge seems overwhelming, tackle it box by box. Such a large endeavor can be less intimidating when done a little at a time. To make progress, set a regular schedule: for example, sort through one box each day or each week. Move it out of the storage area and into another part of the house to examine its contents; when you remove things from their usual context, you're less likely to put them back. Proceeding slowly allows you to consider each item carefully, and gives you the time to digitize photos, documents, or other memorabilia before disposing of them.

And by all means, if you have a storage unit external to your property, get rid of it! It's like renting a second house for your excess stuff–*stuff you don't even like enough to live with.* Ponder the following questions: Can you list the contents of your storage unit from memory? If not, do you really *need* things you don't even know you have? When did you last use these items? Is it worth paying money to store things you never use? If you don't want to keep them in your house, why keep them at all? You may discover that in this situation, the best way to Start Over is to turn in the keys.

DECLUTTER

As you divide your stuff into Trash, Treasure, and Transfer piles, keep it simple and stick to the following rule: if you haven't used an item in over a year, out it goes. This time period is sufficient to cover holiday decorations; seasonal supplies like pool toys and snow shovels; and sports equipment that's only used part of the year, like baseball bats and ice hockey skates. Accordingly, if you didn't go skiing, use your camping gear, or put up those holiday decorations last year (or in several years), it's time to ask *why* you're still storing them.

You'll probably find plenty of stuff for your Trash pile here, as these spaces are often repositories for broken items. Consider how likely you are to fix that old television or lawnmower if you've already replaced it with a new one (I'll give you a hint: not very!). Likewise, question if that chair with the broken seat, or table with the broken leg, will ever enter your dining room again. If you were *really* going to fix these items, you would have done so by now. Break free of the task by letting them go–it'll take a load off your mind, and give you time to pursue other (more pleasurable) activities.

Your Transfer pile will fill up quickly too, as storage spaces are catch-alls for abandoned projects and once-loved hobbies. We often feel guilty for giving up on activities, particularly after we've paid for supplies or training. We then stow the equipment, vowing we'll get back into it someday. Remember, you have no obligation to continue these pursuits. Donate the old table you never finished re-finishing, give your neighbor the fishing pole you haven't touched in years, or sell the sewing machine you never learned to use. Give yourself permission to move on–it's so liberating! When these items no longer weigh on you, you'll have the energy and enthusiasm to pursue new passions.

The same goes for furniture. When we redecorate, we often end up with pieces that no longer "fit"–but instead of setting them free, we stash them away in our garage or basement. If nobody's sitting on them, dining on them, working on them, or sleeping on them, what's the use of keeping them? Baby items in particular are often squirreled away indefinitely, but the only reason to keep those cribs, high chairs, and playpens is if you truly expect to have another child. Don't store that fifteen-year-old stroller because it reminds you of your teenager's more charming years; it doesn't have the power to turn back time. Transfer the items to someone who needs them; let them help out a struggling young family, rather than gather dust in your basement.

Furthermore, don't turn your attic (or basement or garage) into a museum of your past. Turn a critical eye on those yearbooks, swimming trophies, letter sweaters, graduation gowns, and other memorabilia; unless you truly plan to don your football or cheerleading uniform again (and more power to you if you can), free yourself from these artifacts. Give similar thought to any heirlooms hidden here: if they're not special enough to keep in the house, question whether they're special enough to keep at all.

Finally, as you gather up your Treasures, keep this in mind: as wonderful as storage spaces are, they're generally not as clean or climate-controlled as the rest of the house. Dust, dirt, moisture, bugs, and other critters can damage your stuff over time. If and when you do need an item, it may no longer be in tip-top shape, and you'll have to buy a new one anyway. (So much for saving it all those years!) Many wedding gowns–meant to be "passed down" to the next generation–meet a slow demise this way. Make sure your Treasures can survive in this environment. If not, bring them into your main living space for safekeeping, or let someone else use them *now*, rather than let them deteriorate.

Even though it's out of sight, the stuff in our attics, basements, and garages is always there–hanging over our heads, piled beneath our feet, and pressing in on us. Just the thought of being surrounded by junk can be psychologically suffocating. Therefore, Narrow Down the contents of these spaces as much as possible: store only what you regularly use (or expect to in the near future). Don't fill them with "just in cases"–life is more exhilarating when you live with less!

First, reconsider your seasonal decorations. Why devote space to store-bought décor, when nature's bounty is much more elegant? During the holidays, decorate with evergreens, pinecones, and sprigs of holly instead of manufactured baubles. Beautify your home with acorns and leaves in the fall, and fresh and dried flowers in spring. Use pebbles, branches, and fruit–rather than mass-produced tchotchkes–to provide texture and color to your rooms. When you decorate with nature, you have a "fresh" look in every sense of the word–and better yet, nothing to store.

Second, pursue sports and hobbies that require little equipment. You can play soccer and tennis with far less stuff than hockey and football, and you can practice yoga, karate, and dance with next to nothing. You can walk or run in the great outdoors instead of buying a treadmill, and focus on calisthenics instead of exercise machines. Take a similar approach to hobbies: while woodworking, pottery, or metalsmithing are wonderful activities, they require numerous tools and supplies. Learning a language, writing poetry, or sketching may bring you similar satisfaction without all the stuff.

When you decorate with nature, you have a "fresh" look in every sense of the word–and better yet, nothing to store.

Finally, be a borrower. If you only go ice skating once in a while, rent skates instead of owning them; if you only pressure wash your siding once a year, hire the equipment from a home improvement center; if you only need a nail gun once in a blue moon, borrow one from your neighbor. Or join a local tool library to gain access to a wide variety of maintenance and garden equipment. Furthermore, if you rarely use your automobile, sell it and join a car share program–you'll decrease your costs and increase your garage space.

CONTAIN

In these storage areas–as in other parts of the house–it's critical that everything have (and stay in) a designated spot. Haphazard piles of miscellaneous things can swallow up these spaces in no time flat. Resist the temptation to throw something into a corner, or jam it onto the nearest shelf; if you do, you'll end up with a huge, disorganized mess that'll only attract more clutter.

In storage areas–as in other parts of the house–it's critical that everything have (and stay in) a designated spot.

You might assume that everything in these spaces would be Deep Storage, but that's not the case. Our basements and garages contain items we use on a regular basis; therefore, we need to organize the space so the most frequently used ones are within easy reach. In your Inner Circle, store everything you access often–like cleaning supplies, lawn equipment, and tools for home and car repair–on the most accessible shelves, racks, and hooks. Think of your Inner Circle as "active" space, housing all the necessary supplies and equipment (and perhaps even the work area) to perform regular tasks.

Your Outer Circle is primarily storage space–for items used once a year, or part of the year. In this section store your holiday decorations, perishable emergency supplies, and out-of-season maintenance and sports equipment (like your snow blower and skis in summer, or your sprinklers and camping gear in winter). Finally, Deep Storage is for items you have little intention of laying eyes on again, but are obligated to keep for some reason or other. This category shouldn't contain much; in fact, non-perishable emergency supplies, and financial or legal documents are about the only things that come to mind. Most important, don't use Deep Storage to hide things (like heirlooms) that you don't want to deal with.

Because these storage areas house a wide variety of items–from coolers to kayaks, and rakes to roller blades–Modules are the single best way to keep them organized. Consolidate like items, from the largest down to the smallest: in addition to grouping your shovels and rakes, sort your nuts, bolts, and screws by type and size. (For the natural born organizer, it's the stuff of dreams!) Rather than label a handful of boxes "home repair," separate the contents into plumbing, electrical, woodworking, painting, and exterior care Modules.

Likewise, sort decorations according to occasion or season—that way, you won't have to root through your Christmas balls in order to fetch your birthday streamers. Organize sports equipment by activity or participant, and store winter gear (like boots, hats, and gloves) in a separate Module from summer gear (like flip-flops and beach towels). Cull any duplicates or excess in the process.

When something comes in, something goes out—and *not* out to the garage!

Next, find appropriate containers for small to medium-sized items; left on their own, they're apt to wander off and get into trouble. Transparent bins and boxes are ideal, as they enable you to see the contents at a glance. Clearly label or color code opaque containers so you don't have to comb through a dozen boxes to locate what you need. Better yet, take it one step further: make an inventory of each container's contents, print the list, and tape it to the front of the box. With such a system in place, you'll be able to lay your hands on anything in a matter of minutes—as well as keep out any stray items.

Since storage spaces are out of sight, it's tempting to cram them with whatever will fit—but that's not very minimalist, is it? Instead, make liberal use of Limits to keep things under control. First, consider restricting the contents to what will fit on shelving or vertical storage. By taking the floor out of the equation, you'll remove volumes of potential clutter and free up the space for other activities (such as parking your car, working on a hobby, or forming a garage band). Limit your possessions by category as well–like one or two boxes of sports equipment, seasonal decorations, or tools. And if you *must* stow away keepsakes, memorabilia, or other sentimental items, restrict them to a single box.

If we're not careful, our storage spaces can become museums of old technology, retirement homes for old tools, and memorials to old pastimes. Avoid this fate by practicing One-In-One-Out: discard electronics and other items when you replace them with something better, and give up an old sport or hobby (and its related equipment) when you pursue a new one. When something comes in, something goes out–and *not* out to the garage!

MAINTAIN

In your attic, basement, or garage, keep anything that serves as functional space–like workbenches or tables–completely clear. The tasks performed in such areas are sometimes dangerous; therefore, maintaining clutter-free surfaces is an essential safety precaution. In other words, you don't want tennis balls rolling around when you're working with a power saw or handling hazardous chemicals. Furthermore, when you set out to tackle a project, it's discouraging to have to clear the area of junk before you begin. To keep your worktop clear, install a pegboard panel above it; all your tools, screws, nails, bolts, and other bits will then be off the surface, yet within reach.

Likewise, do everything you can to keep the floor clear. These spaces can be awkward and dark, providing a tripping hazard if anything is underfoot. When you're negotiating the terrain with a ten-foot ladder, or fifty-pound bag of rock salt, it's a bad time to discover that your child's wagon is out of place. Make liberal use of vertical storage space, such as shelving and wall-mounted hooks and holders. Hang garden tools like rakes and shovels, sports equipment like skis and skates, and mesh bags of smaller items like soccer balls, helmets, and other accessories. Install overhead racks to stow bicycles and large items out of the way. Ideally, you should be able to walk through the space without stepping over, skirting around, or bumping into any objects.

To maintain clutter-free storage spaces, you *must* be a good gatekeeper–because once stuff settles in, it takes some serious effort to flush it out. Question any item headed for the attic, basement, or garage *before it gets there*; if something's leaving the living space, it can just as often leave the household altogether. Don't use these spaces to avoid facing reality or making tough decisions; if you find yourself walking up the attic steps with your aunt's music box collection, stop and think about alternative ways to deal with it. Giving it to your sister-in-law or donating it to a charity shop may be a better solution than tucking it away.

To maintain clutter-free storage spaces, you *must* be a good gatekeeper.

Additionally, consider doing a one-a-day declutter–these areas provide ample opportunity to purge your household of excess stuff. Better yet, it's *easy*: since the items reside outside your main living space, you're already somewhat detached from them. You don't look at or use them on a daily basis, and you have a pretty good idea of what it's like to live without them. Think of it this way: if you were making a cross-country move, would you bother to drag them along? If they're not special (or useful) enough to wrap up, box up, and cart around, you may as well set them free.

At minimum, conduct a major decluttering session once a year; schedule it on a holiday weekend for a particularly festive atmosphere. Unload the entire contents of the attic, basement, or garage into your backyard for inspection. Purge unused tools, unloved hobby supplies, outgrown sports equipment, and anything else that may have snuck its way in during the previous twelve months. To increase motivation, plan a yard sale for the following week and earmark the proceeds for something fun–like a family vacation or swim club membership. Make it a tradition, and everyone will look forward to the annual fresh start.

28
Gifts, heirlooms, and sentimental items

During the course of your decluttering, you'll come across certain objects that give you pause. They're neither useful nor beautiful, yet you can't bring yourself to discard them. Ironically enough, you may not even have chosen to bring them into your life. What am I talking about? Gifts, heirlooms, and sentimental items.

GIFTS

Gifts are supposed to be good, right? We're supposed to give them with joy, receive them with joy, and cherish them for the rest of our days. Throughout history, gifts have been powerfully symbolic—used to convey respect, curry favor, express love, extend hospitality, seal friendships, ask forgiveness, and more. The key word here is *symbolic*. The gift itself is simply a token of an emotion, intention, or relationship–which, absent that object, remains. In other words, the bond represented by that "Best Friend" mug has little to do with the mug itself.

Unfortunately, modern gift-giving has been overtaken by aggressive marketing. At every major holiday, we're barraged with ads urging us to buy this, that, and the other thing for our loved ones. They promise that happiness will reign if we give our wife the right jewelry, our husband the right gadget, our friend the right scarf, and our children the right toys–and on the flip side, hint at the disappointment they'll suffer if we don't. Consequently, our gift-giving nowadays is often fueled by obligation, expectation, and guilt.

Thanks to such marketing, nary a holiday, birthday, housewarming, wedding, or anniversary goes by without gifts exchanging hands–the evidence of which can be seen in our overstuffed drawers and closets. Multiply these occasions by your number of friends, relatives, and colleagues, and the stuff can build up quickly! Our challenge when we become minimalists is twofold: to purge unwanted gifts we already have and to avoid receiving new ones.

The upside of all these gifts flying around is that most givers quickly forget what they gave you. Can *you* remember what you gave your boss for Christmas, or your spouse for his birthday, two years ago? If so, have you seen it since–and do you care? For most people, the *act* of giving is what's important, and they don't give a second thought to the object after it changes hands. So when your sister-in-law comes to dinner, she probably won't be scanning your shelves for the candle-holder she gave you last year. It's the thought–not the thing–that counts.

Therefore, keep only what you truly love, and set free what you don't–think of it as spreading the giver's generosity into the world! In the future, put unwanted gifts right into your donation box; it's easier to part ways if they don't settle in. Several months will likely pass before you take the contents to charity; if the giver visits in the meantime, retrieve the item temporarily and put it on display. Dealing with long-distance gifts is even easier: express your gratitude with a heartfelt thank-you note, and a photo of the gift in use. Take a selfie wearing that handknit scarf from your cousin or holding that new handbag from your aunt. Send the picture to the giver, and the item to charity, and everyone will be happy.

Alternatively, sell the gift in question and use the money to buy something new. That way, you'll have a symbol of the giver's sentiment in a more functional or beautiful form. You could also re-gift it, if you follow a few simple rules: make sure the item is appropriate for the recipient, and something you would have bought them; re-gift outside the social circle (and preferably region) of the giver; and re-gift only those items you haven't already used.

Better yet–avoid these situations altogether by opting out of gift exchanges. I know, I know–easier said than done! It might be no problem at the office or among casual acquaintances, but it's another story with friends and family. Changing holiday traditions can be a challenge and must be approached with diplomacy and grace. To increase your chance of success, put a positive spin on it: propose spending time together in lieu of gifts, or express a desire to conserve the planet's resources. If a zero gift policy doesn't fly, suggest a Secret Santa or Pollyanna exchange; at least then you'll receive only one gift instead of five, ten, or twenty.

For those who insist on bestowing you with gifts, express your preference for consumables. Tell them how glorious a gift of gourmet cheese, pasta, or coffee beans would be, or mention your sweet tooth, and speak longingly of baked goods and artisan chocolates. Make it known that you love fancy bath salts, hand rolled candles, or scented body lotions. Remind them of your green thumb, and request plants, flowers, or seeds for your garden. Alternatively, suggest "experience" gifts–like music lessons, theater tickets, or membership to a museum. Or propose exchanging gifts of service, like baby-sitting, snow shoveling, a car wash, or computer assistance. Give each other "coupons" for specific tasks, which can be redeemed when needed. Even simpler: have lunch or coffee together to celebrate the holiday.

Better yet, propose charitable donations instead of gifts. The money we spend buying each other gadgets, knickknacks, and tchotchkes can do a world of good for those less fortunate. Instead of shopping, spend an afternoon choosing favorite charities with your loved ones (be sure to involve the kids); the experience can be much more fulfilling than fighting crowds at the mall. Engaging in philanthropy with friends and family brings you closer together for a common cause. It'll make your occasions richer and more meaningful, and you won't have anything to return, re-gift, or declutter.

> Propose spending time together in lieu of gifts.

HEIRLOOMS

When it comes to decluttering, heirlooms are a sticky wicket. In many cases, we would have never chosen to acquire such objects, let alone commit to caring for them the rest of our days. Yet suddenly we find ourselves dusting around Hummel figurines, wondering where to hang a painting of poker-playing dogs, or trying to incorporate a Victorian fainting couch into our contemporary family room. Oftentimes, we don't hold on to these objects because they're useful or beautiful; we keep them out of a sense of guilt, sentiment, and responsibility to preserve our family "heritage."

Heirlooms typically enter our lives when loved ones pass away–that alone can paralyze our decluttering. We feel these objects are all we have left of that special person, and that in letting them go we'll lose that final connection. It's an emotional and difficult process, so give yourself plenty of time to grieve before attempting it. If possible, keep the heirlooms boxed up or stowed away until you're ready to make some decisions; once they settle into your home, it's even more difficult to release them.

The most important thing to remember is that these items were simply things they owned–just like the things you own. Do you feel that you're embodied in your dinner plates, or that your end table symbolizes your being? Of course not! Likewise, your loved one is not the object on your mantelpiece, and shouldn't be equated with it. Do you really think Grandma would want you dusting "her" each week? (Or worse, stashing her in a stuffy attic?) Instead of packing away mementos, honor the person you lost by sharing stories and photographs of them with friends and family. Your memories are infinitely more precious than any "thing" they left behind.

Our obligation is not necessarily to keep the items we inherit, but to find the best use for them. We've been entrusted to steward them to a new home–but it doesn't *have* to be ours. In fact, another relative may be thrilled to own such a piece of family history. Don't let squabbling among heirs compel you to keep things you don't want–in other words, don't hoard the silver serving bowls so your cousin doesn't get them. Graciously pass them along to any takers, and let them be responsible for their safekeeping.

If your heirlooms are valuable or historically significant, lend (or donate) them to a local museum or historical society. Such an institution might welcome the opportunity to display your grandfather's World War I uniform, or your uncle's collection of regional landscape paintings. It's a wonderful way to share your loved one's legacy and transfer the care and responsibility for such precious items into more capable hands. Even if your pieces aren't valuable, try to place them where they'll be appreciated. For example, offer up the grandfather clock or old phonograph you inherited to a nearby retirement home. Give your aunt's doll collection to a little girl who would love it, or donate her boxes of books to the local library. Look for ways these objects can bring joy to others, rather than gather dust in your attic.

Alternatively, sell the items and put the proceeds to good use. Uncle John would probably be thrilled if his sports memorabilia paid for his favorite nephew's baseball camp, as would Aunt Jane be tickled to see her crystal punch bowl finance your new kitchen cabinets. Their intention was not to burden you with musty antiques, but to do something special for you–so all the better if you can transform their generosity into something you'll truly appreciate. Another idea: donate the proceeds to their favorite cause or charity. I'm hard-pressed to think of a better way to honor someone's memory.

If an heirloom has monetary value, treasure it, gift it, donate it, or sell it, but don't hold on to it because it *might* be worth something. We may have fantasies that the stamp collection or oil painting we inherited will fund our retirement, but most often, it's just a handy reason to squirrel it away and avoid dealing with it. Instead of making million-dollar excuses for your clutter, *find out what it's worth*. Search online shops and auctions for similar items to determine its market value. In the process, you'll learn whether your piece is run-of-the-mill or exceedingly rare. If the latter, obtain a professional appraisal, or contact an auction house like Christie's or Sotheby's for an evaluation. But don't despair if you discover that Grandma's "good" silverware sells for bargain basement prices; now you no longer have to drag it around with each move, thinking one day it'll put your child through college. If you keep it, it'll be for its own merits, rather than hope of a future windfall.

No matter their value, sentiment alone will make it difficult to part with some items. But just because you inherited a big collection of pottery doesn't mean you have to keep *all* of it. Choose a special piece (or two), and display it proudly. If the heirloom is a single item, preserve just *part* of it: snip a few squares off that old quilt, or salvage the pulls from that antique dresser. You'll still have something to remind you of its previous owner–it'll just be smaller and easier to store. You can also save the sentiment by digitizing heirlooms. Scan old postcards, letters, documents, and prints, and take digital photos of larger items. A picture of your aunt's treadle sewing machine will bring back the same memories as the item itself–without taking up an inch of space.

Finally, perhaps *you're* planning to pass down some items. It might sound harsh, but keep this in mind: there's a good chance your kids don't want them. They won't have the foggiest idea what to do with your folk art, and your Art Deco sideboard won't fit their décor. If you have valuable items you'd like to bequeath, gauge their interest; they may be happier helping you sell them now than dealing with them later. Make decluttering part of your estate planning–pare down your possessions while you're still here, and don't pass down clutter to the next generation.

SENTIMENTAL ITEMS

Unfortunately, heirlooms aren't the only sentimental items we need worry about; over the course of our lives, we accumulate plenty of our own. Events, milestones, and rites of passage all seem to come with their own "accessories"–and these commemorative items can be tough to get rid of!

We begin accumulating such objects at birth–long before we have a say in the matter. Your parents probably kept your first spoon or baby cup, and may have bronzed your first pair of shoes. They may have stowed away your report cards, swimming trophies, and the pictures you drew in art class. They may have held on to your Little League uniform or Girl Scout badges. As we get older, we pick up the torch: saving our high school yearbooks and graduation gowns, our fraternity (or sorority) memorabilia, ticket stubs from the theater, trinkets from our travels, postcards, greeting cards, letters, and more. Then we get married, have our own kids, and start saving *their* stuff (oh my!).

The memories and emotions attached to these items make them hard to declutter. Parting with them feels like parting with our selves. But we all know that's not true! Discarding your old football jersey won't make you less of an athlete, tossing your wedding favors won't annul your marriage, and purging those baby keepsakes won't make you a bad parent. The events and experiences of our lives are not embodied in these objects. Things are temporary–they can be broken, tarnished, or taken away–but memories last forever.

With that in mind, let's consider some sentimental items that trip us up when decluttering.

Wedding Stuff

Your wedding is one of the most significant and memorable events of your life. However, it can seem like you married not only your spouse, but a whole pile of stuff. You might feel like you've made a lifelong commitment to preserve a dress, train, headpiece, veil, shoes, garter, favors, invitations, flowers, ribbons, cake toppers, serving pieces, centerpieces, guest books, photo albums, frames, cards, candles, decorations, and other keepsakes that entered your life that day. Remember, though: you promised "to have and to hold" your spouse, not boxes full of bridal clutter.

Things are temporary—they can be broken, tarnished, or taken away—but memories last forever.

Use Limits to deal with such items. Choose a handful of pieces for preservation, or reduce your collection to one container. I promise, you won't lose sleep over these trinkets, and your marriage won't suffer a bit. The dress, on the other hand, is a doozy. Wedding gowns are fragile, bulky, and awkward to store, yet we can hardly imagine discarding them. But ponder this: why keep something you'll never wear again? It's probably well-documented in photos or videos, and when you share memories of your wedding, you're more likely to whip out the pictures than the dress.

Are you saving it for your daughter? That's a lovely idea, but she probably won't wear it. (Did you wear *your* mother's dress?) Selecting a dress is a bridal rite of passage; the chance of her choosing a thirty-year-old one from the attic is pretty slim. Furthermore, storage conditions can be harsh on such a delicate garment. While it's still in good condition, sell it, donate it, or alter it–make it into a cocktail dress, or use its fabric for a purse or ring pillow as "something old" on your daughter's wedding day.

Children's Stuff

You could be decluttering like a pro until you come across the pictures your son drew in kindergarten–your heart melts, and your resolve evaporates. It's a parental instinct to save every last item your kids have created–but your children are better served by a spacious environment than piles of old crafts and schoolwork. Still–how can you possibly part with the evidence of their genius?

Limits to the rescue! Instead of saving everything, select the most special and unique pieces. If your "baby" has already left the house, the decisions are yours–but if he's still under your roof, enlist his help. By doing so, you can see what *he* treasures most. At the end of each school year, help your child pick his favorite projects and drawings for his keepsake box. If you like, you can digitize the rejects for posterity, and pass the originals on to grandparents and relatives.

If you're downsizing your empty nest, offer these items to your adult children. If they take them, wonderful! They can decide for themselves what to do with them. If they refuse, then realize this: if such things are of little significance to them, you don't have to keep them either. Your success as a parent is evident in the men and women they are today, not the math homework they did in the third grade. Instead of reminiscing about the past, be part of their lives in the present–and celebrate their current achievements, rather than their former ones.

Handmade Stuff

Hobbies are wonderful outlets for our creativity; sometimes, however, our homes get cluttered with our works of "art." When we're learning a craft, we find that practice makes perfect–and turn out all manner of drawings, paintings, scarves, socks, bowls, stained glass, origami, cards, candles, jewelry, and more while we master the techniques. The problem comes when we can't discard these things simply because *we made them.* But let's be realistic: most of our efforts aren't masterpieces and don't require preservation. Keep only your favorites. As for the rest: give them away, or recycle the materials into new projects.

On the flip side, you may be the recipient of someone else's "art"–like the socks your sister knitted, or the bowl your friend made in pottery class. Graciously accept the item, and use it a few times in the giver's presence (send a photo if they don't live nearby). But if it's not to your taste, don't feel obligated to keep it forever–better for it to be out in the world than stuffed away in your closet. Don't feel guilty; the giver may have been trying to clear out *her* clutter. When you receive such a gift, express your gratitude but don't overdo the enthusiasm–or you'll likely end up with more in the future!

Souvenirs

Visit any famous landmark or monument, and you're sure to see it nearby: the ubiquitous souvenir shop. And more likely than not, it'll be teeming with tourists. For some reason, we feel we haven't really been someplace unless we bring home a tiny replica of it–or a mug, t-shirt, or tote bag emblazoned with its image. Snatching up some proof of our visit seems perfectly natural while sightseeing; it's not until after we get home and unpack that miniature Mount Rushmore that we begin to question our judgment. Too late! That item is now a symbol of our trip, and we're stuck with it forever.

That's not true, of course–our travel experiences have *nothing* to do with tacky trinkets. Tossing that Hawaiian lei or Eiffel Tower paperweight won't erase your honeymoon or that romantic weekend in Paris. Your memories are far more valuable than mass-produced tchotchkes, so purge the tourist clutter without regret. In the future, resist the urge to commemorate your trips with material items; don't feel obligated to buy beer steins in Germany, kimonos in Japan, nesting dolls in Russia, or commemorative key chains from anywhere. If you must bring something home, make it something small: postcards or foreign coins afford ample "evidence" of your travels. Digital photos are even better: they take up no space at all, and provide wonderful documentation of your trip. That said, don't let keepsake-hunting or picture-taking distract you from fully experiencing the places you visit. Your memories make the best souvenirs!

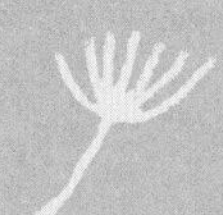

PART FOUR

LIFESTYLE

Now that we've streamlined our stuff, let's take our minimalism a step further. We'll introduce our families to the joy of less, and invite them to declutter along with us. Then we'll discuss how a simpler lifestyle benefits the earth, its inhabitants, and future generations–providing us with even more incentive to reduce our consumption and live lightly on the planet.

29
The clutter-free family

So you've developed a minimalist mindset, mastered the STREAMLINE techniques, and decluttered with success. But as you're basking in your glory, your gaze falls on your toddler's toys or teenager's shoes or partner's pile of paperwork. Uh-oh. . . . You've worked so hard to clear your own clutter, but what about everyone else's?

Don't worry–you *can* live a minimalist lifestyle with a family (even a large one!).

Yes, more people means more clutter. And to complicate matters, the older your loved ones, the less control you have. Your baby won't fuss if you pare down his booties, but it takes a lot more finesse to get your preschooler's plushies or partner's old electronics out of the house.

But take heart–becoming a clutter-free family is doable, and it's worth the effort. In this chapter, I'll give you an action plan that works, whether you're a family of two or ten. These simple steps provide a framework for decluttering a multi-member household–in essence, a family-friendly power boost for the STREAMLINE techniques.

Once we get those down, we'll dive into more detail for specific family members: infants, toddlers and preschoolers, older children, teens, and your spouse or partner. (Spoiler alert: the list goes from least to most challenging.) Every family is different, so feel free to read only what applies to yours–or peruse it all in anticipation of the future.

After reading this chapter, you'll find (perhaps with a sigh of relief) that minimalism and families are not mutually exclusive. In fact, minimalism is not only family-friendly, it's family-affirming. When we clear our homes of all the excess stuff, we can devote our space, time, and energy to the people we love. Now that's something worth working for!

So let's get to that action plan. We're going to set an example, set an agenda, set boundaries, set routines, and set up an Out Box. That's all it takes to apply the STREAMLINE method on a family level. That doesn't sound so hard, does it?

SET AN EXAMPLE

Once you discover the joys of minimalism, it can be hard to contain your excitement. Really, you think, who *wouldn't* want to toss the 80 percent of things they don't use? But your best chance at success is to show before you speak. Evangelizing, pleading, and nagging your loved ones to declutter may well have the opposite effect–and make them more determined to hang on to their stuff.

Instead of mounting a verbal campaign, set an example. Let the serene spaces you've created be your family's introduction to a simpler lifestyle. It may not happen immediately, but over time your spouse will notice that you're less harried and never misplace your keys; your teen will notice that you no longer drag in shopping bags from the mall; your toddler will notice that you spend less time cleaning and more time playing. And that's when you can, ever so gently, begin to ease your family in the same direction.

Furthermore, the experience you gain decluttering your own stuff will help you in assisting your family. Only after you've agonized over *your* things can you understand the issues *they* will face, and only after you've practiced the STREAMLINE techniques (over and over and over again) can you effectively give them the tools they'll need.

Finally, clearing out your own junk will put theirs in the spotlight. When your dining table is piled high with papers, craft supplies, magazines, and toys, nobody knows what belongs to whom. And if *your* clutter has been camouflaging *their* clutter for a while, they may not even realize it's there!

But with yours gone, theirs won't have a place to hide; once it's exposed, you can make a play for its disposal.

After you've conquered your own clutter, it's hard to accept that you can't just take the reins and do the same for your family. But resist the temptation to run around with giant trash bags when everyone goes out; if you want your household to remain clutter-free, your family members have to be partners in the process.

Let the serene spaces you've created be your family's introduction to a simpler lifestyle.

Children in particular learn so much by watching and imitating their parents. Show them that *your* life and happiness doesn't revolve around stuff, and theirs won't either. Don't obsess over buying things, don't spend your weekends at the mall, and by all means, don't cram your own closets and drawers full of excess possessions. Emphasize experiences over things, and family time, nature, and community over consumption. One of my proudest moments as a minimalist mom was when my three-year-old proclaimed, "We don't need lots of toys. We just need the sun."

Above all, be patient. The lightbulb may not go on as quickly for your family members as it did for you. In the meantime, *you* have to be the light–radiating the joys of a simpler lifestyle and illuminating the path forward.

SET AN AGENDA

Now comes the exciting part! With any luck, your joyful decluttering has not gone unnoticed. Whether it sparked a passing comment, some curiosity, or maybe even a little admiration, it's time to invite your family to join in. How you go about this depends entirely on the interest level and enthusiasm they've expressed.

For many, it pays to start small and go slow. Let your partner or kids warm up to the idea slowly as you demonstrate the myriad benefits of lightening your load. Involve them in little decluttering projects to get their feet wet–like cleaning out the hall closet or kitchen junk drawer. Start with easy, communal things to which they have little attachment to develop their capacity to let go.

Others find that going big more effectively lights a fire under their families. Cleaning out the garage or basement builds camaraderie, brings a huge sense of accomplishment, and bolsters confidence for future decluttering. It can be a powerful family bonding experience–an opportunity to celebrate past memories while making space for new ones.

In fact, the solidarity, support, and perspective of loved ones can make a world of difference in the decluttering process. When your son hesitates to let go of his outgrown T-ball equipment, his sister can remind him that he's big enough to play "real" baseball. Or your kids can tell Dad they'd rather hear him play his "good guitar" than the battered one in the garage.

But whether you start small or big, communication is key. When the time is right, have a family meeting–be it a formal affair with the whole brood around the dining table, or an intimate discussion with your spouse–and develop a detailed decluttering agenda.

First, address exactly *what* you hope to accomplish. "Let's declutter" is too vague. Paint the big picture–if you want to empty the dining space so you can sit down to dinner each night, clean out the basement so you can refinish it into a family room, or purge 90 percent of your stuff so you can live on a sailboat, let them know. In order for them to get on board, they need to know the shared goal.

Next, explain *why*. Let them know you'd rather spend weekends hiking together instead of organizing the garage. Let them know you want to have space for them to play without bumping into things. Let them know you want to get out of the house more quickly and calmly in the morning–without a frantic, last-minute search for car keys, backpacks, and school shoes. Let them know you want to have less time for stuff and more time for them.

Finally, outline *how*. Will you work on one closet at a time? Will you clean out the attic over a weekend? Will you have a decluttering contest to see which family member can purge the most stuff? Make a game plan, and give them the tools they need to succeed. Introduce the STREAMLINE techniques–explain how to Start Over, decide what to keep, find a place for everything, use Limits and Modules, pare things down, and implement daily routines to stay clutter-free.

Give each family member a space for their stuff.

Now, you might be wondering–is family consensus needed for *every* discarded item? I say no. If the item in question doesn't belong to a specific person, and has little value (monetary, sentimental, or otherwise), feel free to engage in a little stealth decluttering. If you ask everyone's opinion before tossing the excess cutlery or shabby doormat, someone will surely make a case for keeping it. Make an executive decision, avoid the conflict, and free your family members to focus on decluttering their own things.

SET BOUNDARIES

Remember when you shared a room with your sibling and taped a line down the center to demarcate your territory? Well, that's kind of what we're doing here. It might sound silly, but it's absolutely essential to a clutter-free household.

The key here is to *give each family member a space for their stuff*. This alone should alleviate any immediate panic they feel upon hearing the word "declutter." Emphasize to your loved ones that they don't have to get rid of all their stuff–they just need to keep *their stuff* in *their space*. In essence, it's the Limits technique on a large scale, and makes everyone accountable for their own possessions.

This designated space may be your child's bedroom or playroom, or agreed-upon corner of the family room; your partner's office, hobby room, or portion of the garage (use that tape if you have to!). If you live in a small or open plan home, you may need to get creative, assigning shelves, closets, and sections of rooms to family members. The goal: to keep personal clutter contained and communal space clear.

Initially, this clean sweep of the family space may cause a pile up of clutter in personal spaces. That's okay! Your spouse or kids need to *see* their clutter in order to deal with it. It becomes much more obvious when consolidated (and no longer spread throughout the house). Of course, you don't want your ten-year-old's bedroom to look like an episode of *Hoarders*–that's your cue to step in and help him decide what to keep.

In fact, to get a jump on things, do a little Trash, Treasure, or Transfer during the consolidation process. Your daughter may be content to leave her outgrown dollhouse in the living room for eternity, but would rather toss it than put it in her room. Likewise, your spouse might keep a year's worth of magazines only because it's so convenient to pile them on the dining table. Give them the opportunity to discard what they don't want to take in.

Most important, make sure everyone understands that family space is flex space. In other words, they can play with their toys and read their books and do their craft projects in the living room–but when they're finished, they must take them away (ideally, each evening). You may have to make temporary exceptions now and then, like for the science project on the dining table that's due next week. Just put an expiration date on it so it's not still sitting there when your kid goes to college. Remember, the point of setting boundaries is not to constrict family activities–it's to make space for them!

SET ROUTINES

So if (no, when!) you make it through a successful round of family decluttering, take a moment and celebrate. Tell your partner and kids what a fabulous job they've done, and pause to admire your newly found space (even if it's just some extra room in the coat closet). Treat it as a victory! If decluttering feels fun and positive (instead of like a chore), your family will be inclined to do more of it.

Now put down the champagne glass for a moment, because your work isn't over. Whether you've done a massive purge or a tiny one, you'll need to establish some new routines to prevent a clutter rebound. Please, I implore you, do not skip this step! Systems tend toward entropy, and your home is no different: tomorrow, your daughter will bring home a goody bag from a birthday party, your spouse will haul in something that was on sale, and your son will dump his new rock collection on the coffee table. Don't let this daily onslaught derail your decluttering progress.

Try as you might, you can't stay on top of this alone—these routines must involve the whole family. The first one to implement is an evening sweep of clutter. Choose a period between dinner and bedtime, and have everyone go through the house, gather up their personal items, and return them to their space. Whether it's just you and your partner clearing off the kitchen counter or your family of six dispersing throughout the house, make it a group effort with a clear beginning and end. Yes, you might feel like a drill sergeant at first, but it'll get easier with time. And if done daily (without moaning and groaning), it should take ten minutes, tops.

This evening routine is an incredibly effective way to keep clutter at bay; only so much can pile up in twenty-four hours.

Better yet, the hassle of doing it may open your family's eyes to the drawbacks of "more." More stuff takes more time and more effort to put away each night, whereas less stuff leaves more time for fun. It forces family members to confront their clutter on a daily basis, and may even discourage them from bringing home more of it.

A second routine to introduce: return Everything to Its Place immediately after use. Children can and should learn this as early as possible. Lest you think this impossible, observe a Montessori classroom someday; you'll see children as young as two carefully returning items to their designated spots as soon as they've finished with them.

Finally, it's never too early to implement a One-In-One-Out routine, and make your little one accustomed to giving up an old toy when acquiring a new one. This practice is particularly effective against the gift-tsunamis of birthdays and holidays. By the same token, encourage your teen to give up an old pair of jeans or sneakers when he buys new ones; if parting is such sweet sorrow, he might actually hold off on the purchase until he truly needs them.

Unfortunately, decluttering is not a one-time event that tidies up our lives forever–particularly when we have families. But if you help your loved ones establish new routines for managing their stuff, your home has a much better chance of staying clutter-free.

SET UP AN OUT BOX

Sometimes your home can feel like one big In Box. In come toys, clothing, paper, purchases, gifts, gadgets, and more. Unfortunately, the path back *out* the door isn't quite so clear. To facilitate its departure, you'll need to set up an Out Box. It's easy for stuff to come in, so we need to make it just as easy for stuff to go out.

Let's say the great example you've set has inspired your family to declutter. You've all agreed on an agenda, established your boundaries, and put new routines into place. That's fantastic–until your teenage son wanders into the hallway with some gym socks to discard, has no idea where to put them, and ends up throwing them into a corner of his room to deal with later. The momentum is lost, and the next item may not even make it out his door.

How can you avoid this decluttering failure, and the potential for it to unravel all your hard work? *Make it easy for your family to discard things.* Not save-it-for-the-next-yard-sale easy, but putting-it-in-this-Out-Box-is-easier-than-putting-it-away-easy. No, I'm not suggesting you take advantage of your family's laziness to further your minimalist goals, but sometimes it pays to make decluttering the path of least resistance.

So let's talk more about this Out Box. We want it to be big (so it fits everything), bold (so your family can't miss it), and conveniently located. Of course, size will vary by household and the volume of potential castoffs. Err on the generous side, so the person tossing an old blanket or broken speaker isn't discouraged by a puny box. By bold, I mean make it stand out. Cover that run-of-the-mill cardboard box in bright contact paper, so there's no questioning its purpose. A happy hue will also provide some positive association with the process.

And finally, location, location, location–it's the main factor in an Out Box's success. If you put it in the back corner of the basement or out in the garage, your family may not find their castoffs worthy of the trek. Instead, set it in a central spot that's convenient for everyone–like the mudroom, coat closet, or even the laundry room. Better yet, put it just a few steps from where you think (or hope) most of the clutter will emerge–like the hall closet near your kids' bedrooms or spouse's office.

As head declutterer, you'll have to monitor it (but it's a small price to pay for the potential outflow). Think of it like single-stream recycling: give your family the ease of tossing anything in there, but accept you'll need to sort it in the end.

Why? Because your twelve-year-old might declutter his dress clothes, your teen might declutter her violin, and a mischievous sibling might declutter his sister's favorite teddy bear. (We'll assume your spouse isn't up to any decluttering hijinks!) You want to make sure that all castoffs are intentional and that more valuable ones are dealt with appropriately (that is, sold or donated). Depending on how quickly it builds up, go through the Out Box weekly, monthly, or seasonally–but above all, make sure there's always room for more!

Now that we have a general plan for all families, let's make a more specific one for *yours*. From babies to better halves, this section provides detailed decluttering tips for every family member.

BABIES

Tell your baby about your decluttering plans, and she'll coo, smile, and think it's the best idea she's ever heard!

And she's not just trying to melt your heart–she really is on board with your minimalist agenda. She couldn't care less about the nursery furniture, themed décor, motorized swing, designer bedding, cutesy bath towels, wipe warmer, fussy outfits, musical mobile, or other must-have item from the registry list. All she wants are your loving arms, smiling face, and undivided attention.

For the most part, baby gear is more for the benefit of us new parents (or parents-to-be) than babies. It's sold with the promise to make our (suddenly-turned-upside-down) lives a little easier, more convenient, or more stylish. And when you're feeling nervous and/or clueless, and operating on three hours of sleep a night, you can't part with your money fast enough. (Yes, I'm speaking from experience here.)

Here's my best advice: if your bundle of joy hasn't arrived yet, acquire only the most basic of necessities before birth. Wait until you're in the trenches to see what you *really* need. I promise, all the baby stores won't close their doors the day you deliver, and online retailers will still be offering two-day shipping. So relax, knowing you'll be able to acquire what you need when you need it. Ask for gift cards instead of presents; they're much more useful in the long run.

If your bundle of joy hasn't arrived yet, acquire only the most basic of necessities before birth.

If your newborn's nursery is already filled with everything he'll need until kindergarten, Start Over. Don't make your baby sleep in a storage room. Take it all out, and put back only the things you use on a regular basis. You'll both benefit from a nursery that's soothing, serene, and spacious.

So what exactly do you need in baby's first year? *Your baby will let you know*. (Mine, for example, let me know she hated to be swaddled–after I'd stocked up on a half-dozen swaddling blankets.)

I know, it's not quite the answer you were hoping for (it's much more comforting to have a checklist)–but all babies are different. In hindsight, I could have gotten by with a car seat, a crib, a carrier, and clothing, but I owned more than this (and so will you). Don't fret if you make mistakes; I had a desperate and ill-advised fling with a baby swing that my daughter disliked with a passion. Just chalk it up to a learning experience, donate or sell it, and move on. Keep in mind that, for your baby, space is better than stuff.

And if you haven't done it yet, infancy is the ideal time to minimize your own possessions. When your baby starts to crawl, take his first steps, and motor around the house, you'll realize that decluttering is the best babyproofing. The fewer pieces of furniture to bump into, things to trip over, and knickknacks to knock down, the fewer injuries for him and the more peace of mind for you.

TODDLERS AND PRESCHOOLERS

Things get a little trickier as you enter the toddler years. While you might presume decluttering *carte blanche* over your child, she's developing a desire for control and possession ("no" and "mine" are said to be a toddler's favorite words).

I learned this the hard way. I'd been happily purging anything my daughter hadn't played with in months, assuming she'd neither care nor notice. But around the age of two, she developed a sixth sense for anything that was missing (even if she hadn't touched it in a year).

"Remember my baby rings? I want my baby rings," she demanded the day I packed her stacking rings off to Goodwill. And the afternoon I mailed her outgrown board books to her little cousin, she inquired, "Where's *Baby Colors*? I want to read *Baby Colors*." Three days later, when the request escalated into a full-blown meltdown over the missing book, I made a surreptitious run to the bookstore to re-buy it (not my proudest moment).

It's not the most minimalist of advice, but I recommend a "holding area" for decluttered toddler things–in other words, a place where stuff can stay for an additional few months before it leaves the premises. That way, when your little one notices what's gone, and decides he can't bear to live without it for another minute (cue tears, screams, and rolling on the floor), you'll be able to retrieve said possession without the indignity of purchasing it a second time.

Sometime during the ages of two to five, children develop enough understanding of ownership to realize not everything is "mine"–that things can be shared (temporarily or permanently) with other children. My daughter is fine with relinquishing a toy if she knows where it's going–whether to her baby cousin in Texas, or to "a little girl who doesn't have a lot of toys"–as long as it doesn't just disappear.

In fact, kids this age can be quite eager and proud to pass on their "baby" stuff; take advantage of this enthusiasm to cultivate a love of decluttering! On the other hand, if your little one has a hard time letting go, don't run everything by him; quietly declutter trivial items, and make liberal use of your holding area.

The toddler and preschool years are the ideal time to teach "A Place for Everything, and Everything in Its Place." It takes a little more effort on your part: rather than dumping all their stuff in a toy box, arrange it on shelves where it's easily accessible (and easily returnable). If need be, tape little pictures of the toy to the spot where it belongs–and every time your child plays with an item, help her return it before choosing another.

Use Modules (like bins and baskets) to corral toys with multiple parts (like blocks and puzzles). Again, tape a picture on the container if needed. This strategy not only helps children clean up, it assists with important developmental skills like categorizing and sorting. So there you go–introducing your child to the STREAMLINE method early in life may even make him smarter!

OLDER CHILDREN (AGES 6 TO 12)

Decluttering takes on an entirely new dimension with older children–they're now able to participate fully in the process, and even do some solo streamlining (though I'd still monitor that Out Box). Let the fun begin!

While your preschooler was just beginning to grasp the Trash, Treasure, or Transfer process, your older child is ready to put it into practice. Children of this age love to make decisions. They can clearly discern what belongs in the garbage, what they want to keep, and what they don't want but someone else might. On that last note, they're also developing a sense of empathy and charity, and are often touchingly eager to give their castoffs to a less fortunate child.

The best way to engage teens is to appeal to their sense of emerging adulthood.

Plus, older kids can formulate and articulate a Reason for keeping an item: I like to cuddle with it, it makes me happy, my Nana gave it to me, it makes an awesome siren noise (I didn't say it would be a good reason!). They can also form Reasons for not keeping it: it's broken, it doesn't fit me anymore, I'm too old for it. Talk them through the process; they'll probably get a kick out of having a conversation with their stuff.

They're also better equipped to keep Everything In Its Place. While toddlers still need a lot of assistance, school-age children can put away everything on their own. Better yet–in their quest for independence, they often relish a new responsibility and take pride in a job well done.

Older kids can make their own Modules and will likely enjoy sorting their things into collections. For your part, make sure they have the appropriate containers, and introduce Limits–tell them they can keep all the toy cars (or action figures, or art supplies) that fit into the designated box. They'll probably find it fun to pick favorites and curate their stuff. They're also old enough to understand the One-In-One-Out rule–that to fit a new toy into their box, an old one must leave.

At this age, put Everyday Maintenance routines into full swing. Help your child develop the habit of cleaning up his room each night; it'll keep the mess (and clutter) from getting out of hand, and avoid the inevitable battle when the job becomes overwhelming. It'll also help your child see the value in having less.

TEENAGERS

So, here's the good news–your teen is perfectly able to implement the STREAMLINE method on her own. Once you introduce the techniques, you can step back from the mechanics of decluttering. Your primary role at this age is providing guidance and motivation.

And that's the challenging part–how on earth do you motivate teenagers to pare down their possessions? They're not exactly known for a willingness to please their parents. And therein lies the secret to success: they have to believe they're doing it for themselves, not for you.

My advice, then, is to go big on the first STREAMLINE step: Start Over. Encourage your teen to take everything out of her space, and return only her favorites and essentials. How to spark her enthusiasm? Call it a Room Makeover.

The best way to engage teens is to appeal to their sense of emerging adulthood. They're just a few years away from leaving the nest and may already fantasize about their future lifestyle. The hope is that this opportunity to create their own, more adult space will inspire them to purge their childhood clutter (better to start now than the day they leave for college!).

Just remember to put your sentimentality aside and don't stand in their way. If your teen wants to toss his baseball card collection, or elementary school yearbooks, or gifts from Grandma, let him. If she wants to get rid of her canopy bed and matching dresser, let her. If she wants to declutter the doll collection you painstakingly (and expensively) accumulated for her, so be it.

The point of the Makeover is not to give your teen a decorating budget–far from it! In fact, it should incur little to no expense. The only indulgence I'd encourage is a new paint color, because of the drama value it adds to the transformation. This exercise is not about buying new things, but redesigning their space with their favorite things. To that end, help them apply the STREAMLINE techniques to decide what to keep, where to keep it, and how to keep their new space clutter-free.

When you give your teen permission to discard anything and everything her heart desires, you may be surprised at the minimalist that emerges. In a world where they've been bombarded with marketing and advertising and peer pressure to own more, teenagers may not have the slightest notion that it's acceptable to want less. I've received countless emails from teens over the years, thanking me for the information and support provided on my blog. Some are thrilled to discover minimalism for the first time, some are relieved that an alternative to a work-spend adulthood exists, and some are just desperate to create their own oasis of space in cluttered households.

Just because your teen has a messy room or shops too much doesn't mean she'll never be a minimalist; it may simply be the only thing she's ever known. Introduce her to a simpler lifestyle; the fact that it's against the status quo may very well appeal to her rebellious side. But even if she doesn't embrace it while under your roof, you've given her a wonderful gift. As she makes her way in the world, she'll take with her a powerful example of the joy of less.

PARTNER OR SPOUSE

Finally, let's talk about getting your partner or spouse on the decluttering bandwagon.

If you're just merging households with your partner (or planning to do so), it's the perfect opportunity to Start Over. Don't begin your lives together with two of everything–make short order of culling those duplicates before you settle in. It can be difficult to decide whose toaster or vacuum or sofa is "better"–and as the minimalist, you may have to make more concessions. But paring down before you shack up can make for a much smoother transition.

If you've been living together for a while, you may have a bigger challenge ahead of you. But never fear–it can be done! You might be fortunate and have a partner who embraces the idea wholeheartedly–perhaps they've felt vaguely uncomfortable about the excess stuff in the house, or have even been hinting for *you* to pare down. If this is the case, count your lucky stars and have a blast streamlining together. But even if your partner initially bristles at the thought, don't worry–a little finesse and a lot of patience can turn many a clutterbug into a decluttering ally.

But first things first: hands off their stuff! I know it's tempting, but *do not purge your partner's possessions without their knowledge or permission*–even if you think they won't notice. In your enthusiasm, you might think it kind and expedient to do the hard work yourself, but there's no faster way to build mistrust and defensiveness and dash your chances for success. So take a deep breath, and prepare for a slow, steady, subtle campaign.

It's like cultivating a flower–you need to plant the seed, fertilize it, and drench it in sunlight–but in the end, it must grow and bloom of its own accord.

Let's start with some ways to plant the decluttering seed:

- As we discussed previously, set an example. Truly, there is no better testament to minimalism than a joyful display of it—like a streamlined closet, a beautiful clear countertop, or a kitchen drawer neatly arranged with just the essentials.

- Leave this book in a conspicuous place. Reluctant declutterers may be more receptive to the idea if it comes from a third party. Alternatively, email them articles that might spark interest: about a family that decluttered their way out of debt, or an executive who purged his possessions to pursue a new career path.

- Casually talk about *your* decluttering efforts. Don't open the conversation with, "You have too much stuff"; it'll immediately put them on the defensive. Simply explain how *you're* trying to pare down *your* wardrobe or *your* crafting stash, in the same way you'd talk about a new hobby. It's a great way to introduce the STREAMLINE techniques in an informational (rather than instructive) context.

Once the seed is planted, it's time to fertilize it with the nourishment it needs. You can't get a plant to grow by standing over it and yelling at it—or worse yet, trying to pull it up out of the ground. By the same token, you can't just make somebody do something; you have to inspire them to do it. Here's how:

- Tap into what motivates your spouse. Put yourself in their shoes, and divine what aspect of minimalism would particularly appeal to them. Selling stuff to fund a vacation? Spending less time maintaining things, and more time with the kids? Cutting back on consumption to retire earlier? Emphasize how decluttering will benefit *them*.

- Make it easy. First, agree on spaces where each of you can keep personal stuff and spaces that will remain clutter-free. Then start by discarding trivial, jointly owned items like bathroom toiletries, excess tableware, or office supplies like pens and paperclips. Easy results build confidence in the process.

- Create camaraderie. Remember, you're not in command here, you're working as a team. Solicit your spouse's opinions throughout the process. Instead of declaring that everything in the garage must go, ask, "What do you think is the best way to make more space in here?" They'll be more enthusiastic about the process if they feel equally in control of it. Furthermore, a common goal provides motivation and momentum.

With any luck, your nourishment has produced a nice little seedling–now you must absolutely, positively drench it in sunlight!

- Praise, praise, and praise some more. People love to hear they're doing a good job, and tend to repeat behavior for which they receive positive feedback. If you criticize, on the other hand, you're sure to stop them in their tracks. So even if they only purged a few old t-shirts, don't say "That's all?!" Tell them they're a natural at decluttering and it's wonderful to see some breathing room in their closet. When we believe we're good at something, we want to do more of it.

- Radiate positivity. Maintain a consistently sunny attitude, even when the going gets tough. Don't belittle your spouse if they're finding it difficult to let go of x, y, or z. Sympathize and share some techniques that helped you through the troublesome spots. Avoid arguments, continue to emphasize the benefits, and take a break if things are getting rocky.

- Create a greenhouse effect–in other words, give that seedling optimal growing conditions and shield it from anything detrimental. If your partner's heading out to the mall, suggest a walk in the park together instead. If they're poring over a catalog, distract them with conversation. If they're logging onto eBay, slip into something slinky. You get the idea–turn consumer moments into couple moments, and keep additional clutter out of your home.

Above all, remember to have patience. Clutter doesn't accumulate overnight, and it won't go away that fast (did yours?). Furthermore, it takes time to change long-standing habits and internalize new ways of thinking.

Strong-arming your spouse to declutter quickly is like forcing a plant to flower: sure, you might get instant gratification, but it'll be short-lived. However, if you give the idea a proper growing season and the chance to take root, those seeds of simplicity may grow into a wonderful new way of life.

30
The greater good

Something wonderful happens when we become minimalists: our efforts ripple out to effect positive change in the world. Every time we decide against a frivolous purchase, make do with something we already have, or borrow from a friend instead of buying, it's like giving a little gift to the planet. The air will be a little cleaner, the water a little clearer, the forests a little fuller, the landfills a little emptier. We may have embraced minimalism to save money, save time, or save space in our homes, but our actions have far greater benefits: they save the earth from environmental harm and save people from suffering unfair working conditions. Not bad for wanting some clean closets, huh?

BECOME A "MINSUMER"

Advertisers, corporations, and politicians like to define us as consumers. By encouraging us to buy as much as possible, they succeed in lining their pockets, growing their profits, and getting re-elected. Where does that leave us? Working hard to pay for things we don't need. Putting in overtime to purchase items that'll be obsolete, or out of style, in a matter of months. Struggling to make credit card payments on stuff that's cluttering up our homes. Hmm, something about that doesn't seem quite right. . . .

But here's some wonderful news: minimalist living sets us free! It unshackles us from the "work and spend" cycle, enabling us to create an existence that has little to do with big box stores, must-have items, or finance charges. Instead of toiling away as consumers, we can become "minsumers" instead: minimizing our consumption to what meets our needs, minimizing the impact of our consumption on the environment, and minimizing the effect of our consumption on other people's lives.

Becoming minsumers doesn't mean we can never set foot in a store again. I don't know about you, but I'm not that comfortable foraging or dumpster diving for the stuff I need–and I certainly don't expect to get anything for free. I appreciate the ease with which we can obtain basic necessities, and the fact that (unlike our ancestors) we don't have to devote our days to securing food, clothing, and shelter. However, I believe that once these needs are met, consumption can be put on the back burner. Once we're warm, safe, and fed, we shouldn't feel compelled to browse a shopping mall or surf the Internet to find *more* things to buy. Instead, we could devote that time and energy to other, more fulfilling pursuits–such as those of a spiritual, civic, philosophical, artistic, or cultural nature.

So what do we have to do to become minsumers? Not much, actually. We don't have to protest, boycott, or block the doors to megastores; in fact, we don't even have to lift a finger, leave the house, or spend an extra moment of our precious time. It's simply a matter of *not buying*. Whenever we ignore television commercials, breeze by impulse items without a glance, borrow books from the library, mend our clothes instead of replacing them, or resist purchasing the latest electronic gadget, we're committing our own little acts of "consumer disobedience." By simply *not buying*, we accomplish a world of good: we avoid supporting exploitative labor practices, and we reclaim the resources of our planet. It's one of the easiest and most effective ways to heal the earth and improve the lives of its inhabitants.

REDUCE

We're all familiar with the phrase, "Reduce, Reuse, Recycle." Of the three "R's," Recycling is the superstar, highlighted in environmental campaigns and community programs. When we decide to go "green," this is usually the focal point of our efforts. Reducing, however, is the unsung hero of this trinity–because the less we buy in the first place, the less we need to recycle! Reducing neatly sidesteps the entire resource-, labor-, and energy-intensive process, and is therefore the cornerstone of our minsumer philosophy.

The best way to reduce is to buy only what we truly need.

Every product we buy involves three important steps in its life cycle: production, distribution, and disposal. In the production phase, natural resources and energy are used to make the item. In some cases, harmful chemicals are released into the air and water as a byproduct of the manufacturing process. In the distribution phase, energy (typically in the form of oil for trucks, ships, and airplanes) is used to transport the item from factory to store, which often means a trip halfway around the world. In the disposal phase, the item has potential to clog our landfills and leach toxins into the environment as it degrades.

By recycling, we're trying to do some damage control–by avoiding the problems of disposal and reusing materials to make new goods. Reducing, on the other hand, eliminates the entire troublesome process altogether. Each item we *don't buy* is one less thing to be produced, distributed, and disposed of. Better to never own the item in the first place than have to worry about how it was made, how it got here, and how to get rid of it later on.

The best way to reduce is to buy only what we truly need. Rather than shopping mindlessly, we must *think* about every purchase—whether it's clothing, furniture, electronics, décor, or even food. We should develop a habit of asking "why" before we buy. For example: am I purchasing this because I really need it, or because I saw it in an ad, on a friend, or looking pretty in the showcase? We should stop and consider whether we could get along just as well without it. In fact, regard a line at the register as a blessing in disguise, as it gives you ample time to evaluate what's in your shopping cart. I've walked away from many a checkout counter after pausing to reflect on potential purchases.

The techniques you can use to reduce your consumption are countless. Enjoy the challenge of meeting your needs in alternative ways, and cobble together a creative solution instead of running to the store. It can be as easy as borrowing a tool from a neighbor, or as resourceful as devising your own drip irrigation system from materials you have on hand. Additionally, favor multipurpose items over single-use ones. A simple vinegar and water solution can eliminate the need for a plethora of commercial cleaners, and versatile clothing can be dressed up or down to suit any occasion. Finally, don't replace something that works simply because you want a new one–be proud of keeping your old car going, or getting a few more years out of your wool coat.

REUSE

The second "R," Reuse, is also central to our minsumer efforts. The longer we can keep a particular item in service, the better–especially if it prevents us from having to buy something new. Since resources have already been devoted to its production and distribution, we have a responsibility to get the most use possible from it.

Like reducing, reusing is preferable to recycling. While recycling requires additional energy to make something new, reusing requires none. We simply adapt the product, in its original form, to meet different needs. My reuse hero is Scarlett O'Hara; if she could fashion a gorgeous dress from some old curtains, we can certainly make seedling planters from our yogurt cups and rags from our old t-shirts. We don't even need to be *that* creative. We have plenty of opportunities to reuse things on a regular basis: like the packaging materials we receive (boxes, bubble paper, packing peanuts), and the wrapping paper, ribbons, and bows on our gifts. In fact, before you toss a glass jar, Christmas card, or takeout container into the recycling bin, consider if you can repurpose it for something else you need.

Of course, as minimalists, we don't want to clutter our drawers and cabinets with stuff we might *never* use. Therefore, if *you* don't have need for something, give it to someone who does. Reuse doesn't necessarily mean that *you* have to reuse it; the planet will be just as well off if somebody else does. To this end, sell your old stuff or give it away. Ask friends, family, and colleagues if they can use your castoffs. Offer up your excess to local schools, churches, shelters, and nursing homes. Finding another home for something takes a little more effort than putting it out on the curb; however, it keeps perfectly useful items in circulation longer and keeps someone else from having to buy new.

By the same token, consider reusing someone else's stuff for *your* needs. Suppose you've been invited to a wedding and don't have an appropriate outfit. Before you hit the department stores, try to find something pre-owned: check out the thrift stores and charity shops in your area, and search online auctions and classifieds. Failing that, raid the closets of friends and relatives, or make use of a rental service. Do the same for tools, furniture, electronics, and almost anything you can think of; regard the secondhand market as your default source, and only buy retail as a last resort. You'll avoid putting additional pressure on our overtaxed environment, and prevent something useful from winding up in the trash.

RECYCLE

Our ultimate goal as minsumers is to live lightly on the earth. Our primary strategy is to Reduce our consumption to the bare bones, and our second is to Reuse whatever we can. However, we'll still sometimes end up with items that are no longer useful, and in those cases, we should make every effort possible to Recycle them.

Fortunately, recycling has become much easier in recent years. Many communities operate curbside programs for picking up glass, paper, metal, and some plastics. Others maintain drop-off stations for recyclable materials. If such resources are available to you, take advantage of them. We want to minimize not only the junk in our homes, but also the junk in our environment.

In fact, don't limit your recycling efforts to the usual suspects–investigate the prospects for other items as well. Some office supply and electronic stores offer "take-back" services for computers, monitors, peripherals, printers, fax machines, cell phones, and personal electronics. Other companies offer mail-in programs, with prepaid boxes or shipping labels, for returning used products. When I replaced my laptop, I was thrilled to be able to send my old one back to the manufacturer. Look around, and you'll find programs for recycling eyeglasses, shoes, furniture, batteries, printer cartridges, clothing, carpets, mattresses, lightbulbs, and more. Before you put *anything* in the trash, take some time to research recycling options. You may be surprised by the possibilities.

You can even do some recycling in your own backyard. Instead of bagging up your leaves, twigs, grass clippings, pine needles, and other yard waste for the garbage collector, start a compost pile. Add kitchen scraps like vegetable matter, coffee grounds, tea bags, and eggshells to the heap; when everything decomposes, you'll have a wonderful, organic substance with which to enrich your garden soil. Consult a gardening book or website for a complete list of eligible waste, and to learn how to layer and stir the materials. Composting is doubly good for the environment: it keeps trash out of the landfill and eliminates the need to buy packaged, commercial fertilizer.

Our ultimate goal as minsumers is to live lightly on the earth.

Although recycling occurs at the end of a product's life cycle, keep it in mind from the very beginning. When you're shopping, favor products that can be recycled over those that can't; they're usually marked with the universal recycling symbol. Different plastics are identified by the number inside the symbol; make sure the particular type is recyclable in your community. If not, consider a more eco-friendly alternative. Likewise, avoid acquiring hazardous and toxic materials (like paints, cleaners, and pesticides). Improper disposal of such items is harmful to the environment, and you'll need to drop them off at special collection sites to get rid of them. Take the easy way out, and seek nontoxic products to meet your household needs.

CONSIDER THE LIFESPAN

As minsumers, we aim to purchase as little as possible; therefore, we want the stuff we buy to last a long time. We must consider the lifespan of an item in our decision to acquire it. Why waste all those precious resources–for production, distribution, and disposal–on a product we have for just a few months?

For this reason, favor items that are well made and durable. That sounds like a no-brainer, but how many times have you let price, rather than quality, influence what you buy? When you're shopping, it's easy to compare prices, but it can be difficult to determine quality. How do you know if that chair will collapse next month, or if that watch will stop ticking next week? You have to put on your detective hat, and look for clues: like where the product was made, the materials out of which it's constructed, and the reputation of the manufacturer. Although price isn't always a gauge of quality, low cost isn't typically associated with longevity, and while replacing the item may not break the bank, we must consider the environmental costs of doing so.

Accordingly, refrain from purchasing trendy items. These things will never wear out before you tire of them (or before you're too embarrassed to own them). Even if you donate them, resources were still wasted on their manufacture and distribution–better to have never purchased them in the first place. Instead, choose pieces you truly love, or classic items that'll stay in style forever.

Finally, avoid disposable products whenever possible. We certainly don't want to deplete our natural resources on items we use for *minutes!* Unfortunately, "single-use" stuff has become increasingly popular in our society: from plates to razors, napkins to diapers, cameras to cleaning cloths. Many such items are used daily and generate a tremendous amount of waste. You can slash your carbon footprint dramatically by favoring reusable versions, such as handkerchiefs, canvas shopping bags, rechargeable batteries, proper tableware and utensils, and cloth napkins, diapers, and towels. As always, let the lifespan of a product be your guide; if it's ridiculously short, look for a longer-lasting alternative.

CONSIDER THE MATERIALS

When evaluating a potential purchase, give due consideration to the materials from which it was made. By choosing items produced with sustainable or renewable resources, you can minimize the impact of your consumption.

As a general rule, favor products made from natural materials over man-made ones. Synthetic substances like plastics are typically made from petroleum, which is a non-renewable resource. Not only is the manufacturing process energy-intensive; it can emit harmful toxins, and expose workers to hazardous fumes and chemicals. Furthermore, some plastics contain additives that can leach into food and water and pose a health risk. Disposal presents an additional problem. Plastics degrade very slowly, and can persist in landfills for hundreds (or even thousands) of years; burning them, on the other hand, can create toxic pollution.

Natural materials don't require the same energy inputs, and are significantly easier to dispose of and recycle. But just because we're buying something made of wood doesn't mean we're in the clear. We must still be vigilant with regard to its origin and harvesting. Large swaths of land have been deforested to produce paper, furniture, flooring, lumber, and other products. Illegal logging and unsustainable harvesting have destroyed ecosystems, displaced indigenous tribes, and altered local climates. To avoid contributing to such tragedies, look for wood that has been certified as coming from sustainable sources, and favor rapidly renewable types (like bamboo) over endangered species.

Alternatively, reduce your environmental impact by purchasing products made from recycled content. You'll find paper, clothing, handbags, shoes, flooring, furniture, décor, jewelry, glassware, and plenty of other items that are enjoying a second life as something new. Buying recycled goods preserves natural resources, saves energy, and prevents the original items from ending up in a landfill. Show your true minsumer spirit, and take pride in the fact that your tote bag was made from soda bottles, or your dining table from reclaimed wood.

Finally, consider the packaging. The ideal, of course, is none at all–especially considering the brevity of its lifespan. However, many of the items we buy will come with some sort of outer casing. Favor those products with the least amount of packaging, or packaging that can easily be recycled. And by all means, don't bring home your purchases in a plastic bag; make it a habit to use cloth ones instead. This action alone can save a significant amount of energy and waste.

CONSIDER THE PEOPLE

Not only must we evaluate the materials from which a product was made; we must consider who made it, and under what conditions. That tchotchke on the department store shelf or that dress on a retailer's rack didn't materialize out of thin air. Some person either constructed it by hand, or operated the machinery to do so. Before we buy it, we want to know if that person was treated fairly, provided with safe working conditions, and paid a livable wage.

In my world-of-the-future fantasies, I imagine being able to scan the barcode of a product with my phone to discover its history: like what natural resources were used in its production; whether it can be recycled, or how long it will take to degrade in a landfill; where it was made; and the manufacturer's track record with respect to wages and working conditions.

Research the retailers and brands you patronize to make sure their practices are in line with your values.

Decades ago, such information was easy to obtain. Factories were located in our towns and cities, and we could see with our own eyes whether smokestacks were belching out pollution, or chemicals being dumped into lakes and rivers. We could visit the factory floor, or ask our neighbor, cousin, or friend who worked there if they were treated properly and paid adequately. We could trust that unions, laws, and regulations ensured a fair wage and safe environment for the people who made our stuff. With the advent of globalization, all that changed. Most of the things we buy now are made in far-flung locales, and companies are rarely transparent about their supply chains or production methods. Some use foreign subcontractors for their manufacturing, and may themselves be unaware of the conditions under which their products are made.

So how will we know? Well, that's the tricky part. Obviously, no company is going to put out a press release on how little they pay their workers, or run commercials showing the miserable conditions in their factories. We must take it upon ourselves to learn which manufacturers employ fair labor practices and which ones don't. Search the Internet for information from watchdog groups and human rights organizations. Research the retailers and brands you patronize to make sure their practices are in line with your values; if they're not, take your business elsewhere. Also, inspect the origin label before you buy something–if the product was made in a region known for environmental destruction or exploited labor, pass up the purchase and move on.

CONSIDER THE DISTANCE

We've talked a lot about production and disposal, and how we can minimize our footprints with respect to them. But we're not done yet. We must also consider distribution–and how the transport of goods from where they're made to where we buy them adds to their environmental toll.

Once upon a time, the majority of our goods were produced close to our homes. We bought our vegetables from the farmer who raised them, our clothes from the tailor who sewed them, and our tools from the blacksmith who forged them. In most cases, such items traveled no more than a hundred miles (and usually quite a bit less) to reach us. Now, our stores carry produce from Chile, apparel from India, and hardware from China. Much of the stuff in our households originated halfway around the globe. The problem: the additional energy (in the form of fuel) that must be expended to transport it.

Oil is a non-renewable energy source that gets scarcer by the minute. Yet, instead of conserving it, we fill up planes, ships, and trucks with it to move consumer goods from one corner of the world to another. Unfortunately, that means more pollution in our atmosphere and less resources in our future. Is it really worth the environmental consequences to send a mango, or a miniskirt, on a three-thousand-mile journey?

Not to us minsumers. We prefer to buy our goods locally, keep our air cleaner, and save all that energy. We'd rather purchase our chairs from a local craftsperson than a furniture superstore; our décor from the community arts fair instead of a global retailer; and our clothes from a manufacturer in our own country. It's certainly not as easy as popping into the megamart, but the least we can do is *try*. In fact, the more we demand domestic goods over imported ones, the more likely we'll see a revival in local manufacturing.

Ready to do some short-distance shopping? Start with food. Many of us have access to local farmers' markets where we can purchase fresh fruits, vegetables, honey, meats, dairy products, and more. Since the items are grown, raised, and produced locally, the energy expended in transportation is minimal. Therefore, plan your menu according to what's in season. Instead of buying tomatoes in winter from some far-off land, enjoy the fruits of your local harvest throughout the year.

When we buy local, we not only save the environment, we also strengthen our communities. Instead of sending our hard-earned dollars to foreign nations, we put them right back into our own neighborhoods–where they can provide the services, build the infrastructure, and fund the programs we need. We save our farmland from developers, thereby preserving open space and agricultural traditions. We foster strong and diverse local economies, which are far less dependent on global markets and supply chains. Best of all, we build long-lasting, personal relationships with the people who supply our stuff. It's wonderful to know that our consumption is helping a farmer maintain his livelihood, or a local merchant's child attend college–rather than paying the bonus of some distant corporate executive.

BE A BUTTERFLY

When we overconsume, we're like bulls running through a china shop–leaving a destructive path of downed forests, dirty waterways, and overflowing landfills in our wake. In our quest for more goods and unfettered growth, we break the earth's fragile ecosystems and leave future generations to clean up the mess.

As minsumers, we want to do the opposite. Instead of being bulls, we strive to be butterflies–living as lightly, gracefully, and beautifully as possible. We want to flit through life with little baggage, unencumbered by excess stuff. We want to leave the earth and its resources whole and intact.

We inspire others with the beauty of our actions.

The earth has a finite number of resources for a growing number of people, and as more countries become industrialized, the greater the pressure on the system. When we act like bulls, we grab more than our fair share. We feel entitled to support our consumer lifestyles at any cost, and worry little about the effects on the environment. What's worse: in a growth at all costs economy, such behavior becomes the norm. Imagine hundreds, thousands, even millions of bulls stomping through the world and stripping it of its bounty.

When we act like butterflies, on the other hand, we're satisfied with the barest of essentials. We consume as little as possible, conscious of the fact that resources are limited. We celebrate the gifts of nature–a spring breeze, a clear stream, a fragrant flower–rather than trampling them. We're aware that we're stewards of the earth and have a responsibility to nourish and nurture it for future generations. We exist harmoniously with each other, and within the ecosystem.

Furthermore, we inspire others with the beauty of our actions. We don't need power or money to further our agenda; we simply need to do what we do, day in and day out, and set a wonderful example for our neighbors and our children. By embracing minimalist living, we have a unique opportunity to change the current paradigm from one of overconsumption and profiteering to one of conservation and sustainable growth. We can be pioneers of social and economic change simply by consuming less, and encouraging others to do the same. It's the easiest form of activism imaginable, yet has the power to transform our lives, our society, and our planet.

Conclusion

Everyone has their own reasons for embracing a minimalist lifestyle. Perhaps you picked up this book because your drawers are stuffed, your rooms are cluttered, and your closets are bursting at the seams. Perhaps you realized that shopping at the mall and constantly acquiring new things isn't making you happy. Perhaps you're concerned about the effects of your consumption on the environment, and worried that your children and grandchildren won't have the clean air and water that should be their birthright.

I hope that the advice in these pages has inspired you to declutter your home, simplify your life, and live a little more lightly on the earth. It's a message you won't hear very often in our "more is better" society; in fact, you'll almost always hear the opposite. Everywhere we turn, we're encouraged to consume–by commercials, magazines, billboards, radio, and ads on buses, benches, buildings, bathroom stalls, and even in our schools. That's because traditional media outlets are largely controlled by people who profit when we buy more stuff.

Practicing a minimalist lifestyle can sometimes feel like you're swimming upstream. You'll encounter people who feel threatened by any deviation from the status quo; they'll say you can't possibly get by without a car, a television, or a full suite of living room furniture. They'll imply that you're not successful if you don't buy designer clothes, the latest electronic gadgets, and the biggest house you can afford.

Don't believe it. We all know that quality of life has nothing to do with consumer goods and that "stuff" is not a measure of success.

And don't worry–you're not going it alone. Look beyond big media and you'll find plenty of kindred souls. In fact, mention offhand to your colleague or neighbor that you're downsizing your possessions, and you'll likely be met with a knowing sigh and a comment to the effect of "I'd like to do that, too." After the economic excesses of the last few decades, there's a growing disillusionment with consumerism and a groundswell of interest in living simpler, more meaningful lives.

The Internet in particular is a treasure trove of information and support. In recent years, the number of blogs and websites about minimalist living and voluntary simplicity has increased exponentially. Consider participating in a discussion forum on the topic; it's a great way to connect with fellow minimalists, trade decluttering techniques, and find inspiration and motivation to continue on the path.

Once you've stepped outside the status quo, you'll feel a wonderful sense of calm and serenity. When you ignore advertisements and minimize your consumption, there's no reason to long for items, no pressure to buy them, and no stress to pay for them. It's like taking a magic wand and eliminating a host of worries and problems from your life.

With minimalist living comes freedom–freedom from debt, from clutter, and from the rat race. Each extraneous thing you eliminate from your life feels like a weight lifted from your shoulders. You'll have fewer errands to run and less to shop for, pay for, clean, maintain, and insure. Moreover, when you're not chasing status symbols or keeping up with the Joneses, you gain time and energy for more fulfilling pursuits: like playing with your kids, participating in your community, and pondering the meaning of life.

Such freedom, in turn, affords a fabulous opportunity for self-discovery. When we identify with brands and express ourselves through material items, we lose our sense of who we are. We use consumer goods to project a certain image of ourselves–buying a persona, in essence, to show to the rest of the world. Furthermore, we're so busy dealing with *stuff*–running to and fro, buying this and that–that we find little time to stop and explore what really makes us tick.

When we become minimalists, we strip away all the excess to uncover our true selves. We take the time to contemplate who we are, what we find important, and what makes us truly happy.

We emerge from our cocoons of consumerism, and stretch our wings as poets, philosophers, artists, activists, mothers, fathers, spouses, friends. Most important, we redefine ourselves by what we do, how we think, and who we love, rather than what we buy.

There's an old Buddhist story about a man who visited a Zen master, seeking spiritual guidance. Instead of listening, however, the visitor spoke mainly of his own ideas. After a while, the master served tea. He filled the visitor's cup, and then kept pouring as it spilled over onto the table. Surprised, the visitor exclaimed that the cup was full–and asked why he kept pouring when nothing more would fit. The master explained that like the cup, the visitor was already full of his own ideas and opinions–and that he couldn't learn anything until his cup was emptied.

The same thing happens when our lives are too full. We don't have room for new experiences and miss out on chances to develop ourselves and deepen our relationships. Becoming minimalists helps us remedy this. By purging the excess from our homes, our schedules, and our minds, we empty our cups–giving us infinite capacity for life, love, hopes, dreams, and copious amounts of joy.